The
Four Faces
of Woman

Restoring Your Authentic Power,
Recovering Your Eternal Beauty

First published by O-Books, 2008
Reprinted, 2011
O-Books is an imprint of John Hunt Publishing Ltd., Laurel House, Station Approach,
Alresford, Hants, SO24 9JH, UK
office1@o-books.net
www.o-books.com

For distributor details and how to order please visit the 'Ordering' section on our website.

Text copyright: Caroline T. Ward 2008

ISBN: 978 1 84694 086 6

A CIP catalogue record for this book is available from the British Library.

Design: Stuart Davies

Cover Design: Marcia Grace

Illustrations of Shakti Archetypes: Marie Binder

8 Powers: drawn from Brahma Kumais teachings.

Printed in the UK by CPI Antony Rowe
Printed in the USA by Offset Paperback Mfrs, Inc

We operate a distinctive and ethical publishing philosophy in all
areas of our business, from our global network of authors to
production and worldwide distribution.

The Four Faces of Woman

Restoring Your Authentic Power,
Recovering Your Eternal Beauty

Caroline T. Ward

BKIS

BOOKS

Winchester, UK
Washington, USA

CONTENTS

Part 2 - How it Shows up in Daily Life

Seed, Essence, Original Form
I am:
The Eternal Face

Graft, Adaptation, Conform
I am who you say I am:
The Traditional Face

Hybrid, Resistance, Reform
I am not who you say I am:
The Modern Face

Gardener, Renewal, Transform
I access the power to be who I am:
Shakti - The Face of Spiritual Power

Dedication

To that One, the Divine, god who is the Comforter of my Heart, the Source... for guiding me daily and opening my mind and my heart gently and insistently.

To Dadi Prakashmani whose light was so pure, so bright, she revealed God.
To my mother Joan, who through her courage to find her way home to herself, modelled for me the hope which is everpresent in life.

A Special Thanks

Many of stories in this book have been lived and told by women from all over the world. To honour their trust, I have changed names and sometimes even places. But the stories are theirs and my gratitude is to them for sharing them with me.

ACKNOWLEDGEMENTS

A Place of Spiritual Learning

Apart from learning from almost everyone I have the privilege to meet in my life, I need to acknowledge that a great deal that is written in this book, its stories, insights and teachings is drawn from the wisdom shared at the Brahma Kumaris World Spiritual University. My learning with the BKs for almost 20 years has inspired in me a way of seeing the world that takes into account the subtle, the unseen, the hand of God. Some things are directly from the Brahma Kumaris teachings, such as The 8 Powers; others are more tacit connections. I am eternally grateful to the selfless guidance I have received all these years.

Individuals

The first note of gratitude is to Helen Chapman, the woman who conceptualized the idea the Four Faces and whose humble inspiration has liberated many of us. To the team who designed and organized the original meeting in India in 1996 – BK Dr. Nirmala Kajaria, Helen Northey, the wonderful and late Dawn Griggs, Christine Westbury, Amanda Quinn, Lenny de Vries and Yaja Nowakowski.

Eternal appreciation to Angelica Fanjul, Marilén Wood and Maribel Vidal who ensured this book was published in the first place – albeit in Spanish! Also to the Four Faces team in Chile – Lucia, Cecilia, Claudia and Klaus, to Adriana and Gladys, to the entire BK community, the translation team and all there who helped this to happen.

The list of people to acknowledge is vast – the following is not complete by any means complete, Dadi Janki and Dadi Gulzar, Valerianne from Geneva, Sally, Marcia, Chrissy and Silvana from Australia, Luciana, Patricia, Marcia, Flavia and the team from Brazil, Colleen for taking on the website, Rose and Rachel, Anne, Rani and Armelle from France, Isabelle, Judy and

Tanya from Canada, Njeri, Sheetal, Wangui and Angela from
Kenya, Morni and Devi from Hong Kong, Marie-Lisette and Alice
from Holland, Karin, Els and Marga from Belgium, Irene and Pat
from USA, Jill from New Zealand, Moira, Agustina and Gabriela
from Argentina.

I would also like to thank my old friend Mary Anne Williams
who generously detailed her way through this manuscript to
make sure it was making sense!

THE BEGINNING

My spiritual alarm clock went off when my partner was diagnosed with terminal cancer. Michael and I had been together just five months at that time and we were only together for another five months before he died. However those next five months expanded to embrace a lifetime, or perhaps many lifetimes, of experience. From the two of us living a 'party life' in the entertainment industry, our lives transformed overnight.

During the final five months we learned meditation, we ate well, got up at 4am instead of going to bed at that time. We came to 'see' a life neither of us had ever seen before. We came to 'feel' a world that we hadn't known existed. A veil was removed from our senses and we came to life... even as Michael was dying.

It was an extraordinary time in which I learned truly what commitment means, what love is and how important compassion is in a world without mercy. Of course there were difficult moments, but overall we were blessed.

Ten days before Michael died, I realized it was over, I couldn't save him, or keep him with me. It was my rock bottom. Whilst falling apart I finally surrendered knowing that I couldn't control things, I couldn't fix it no matter how strong my wish or my will.

As I sat upstairs in our friend Judy's meditation room, with physical pain in my chest, sobbing my eyes out, I remember saying to God, "Alright God, I don't know who you are or what you do for a living, but this is too hard, I can't do it anymore, *you* have to do it."

In that moment I was born to another knowing. All sorrow ceased – the pain, the sobbing, the fear. In the letting go I was cocooned in the most exquisite love I had ever experienced. In surrender, I was caught, held, in the gentlest and most potent peace possible.

And then I was given guidance... very clearly. The thoughts were as if someone were speaking directly into my mind. "You don't own this soul, you are like two actors who have come together to play a scene. You don't have to know the next scene, you just have to play this one the best that you can. And the way to do that, is to find the joy in every moment."

This was my first 'experience' of God, of something Divine and beyond mere belief or doctrine. When I shared this experience, there were some who tried to tell me that it wasn't God, it was the best of me. That was very nice of them, but I know the best of me had already emerged in the months prior to this point. So I knew the difference between what emerged from within, and what was a gift of grace from without.

And the gift transformed my life forever.

When Michael left, I was privileged enough to be lying beside him in our bed at home. I felt the gentle grace surrounding him as he gathered up his light from within his failing body. His last breath... a moment that expanded to contain eternity as he held still to love me one more time. Then from my heart the word "fly..." emerged ... and he did.

The weeks that followed were mostly blissful. Grace had entered my life and it remained. Occasionally I found myself deeply sad for the possibilities which had been snatched away with an accompanying thought of "It's not fair". I didn't entertain this thought, usually dismissing it as un-useful thinking. I shared this one day and one of my sisters said, "Don't you think you're in denial?"

Oh my God, I thought, I'm in denial! So the next time the thought came, I decided to follow the path of the thought. Within two minutes I was inexorably, emotionally tragic. It took me hours to recover, and what did I achieve? It wasn't real, it was a constructed experience from a series of thoughts that came from a very powerless state. What was fair anyway? Life is. It happens and if you want to, you can find the magic. Besides, I was not powerless.

Michael had given me an extraordinary gift, perhaps even

greater than had he stayed with me. We both knew we were lucky, even in those last months we would connect so deeply through the eyes and marvel at how lucky we were. And we really were.

His physical unwellness gave us both a window to the unseen, a doorway to spirit... as he left, he handed me a path to my own truth and empowerment.

I still feel lucky. My life today is so radically different from the life I lived before I knew Michael, that people often ask me how I ended up where I am – a seemingly quantum leap from where I was twenty years ago. Now that I understand The Four Faces, everything makes sense – the spontaneity, the hope, the sorrow, the strength, the struggle, the surrender, the freedom, the power, the love, the grace – it is the journey of the soul.

I came to see that while many things happen in life, they are not separate from me. They are not random. I started to understand the relationship between my inner world – my thoughts and feelings – and the results that showed up in my outer world. This was both challenging and empowering. Challenging because I could no longer blame anything or anyone for my circumstances and empowering because I realized that my life was totally in my hands.

I even reframed the feelings of hopelessness, restlessness and discontent... they were no longer categorized as depression. The voice of my spirit was waking me up, calling out for a return to my own self, my original true nature, my Eternal Face.

What are the Four Faces of Woman?

These faces are ones that we all know. They live within us and through us. They give us beauty and strength, love and compassion, freedom and the promise of freedom, security and the illusion of security.

The Eternal Face whispers to us of our original self, the seed of who we are – authentic power, innocence, pure love, peace and joy.

The Traditional Face convinces us that safety and success comes from defining ourselves through the eyes and beliefs of others.

The Modern Face finds the courage to reject the imposition of others, seeking to return to the truth of who we are.

The Shakti Face – the face of spiritual wisdom and power – is the key to return to our true self without the struggle and cost of the Modern Face.

Why women?

Over the years, I have been challenged many times that these faces belong to both men and women... and I'm certain that they do.

However, I was just two years on my spiritual path when the vision came to me. It signaled that I must somehow work with women. And as I started to gather with women, sharing spiritual stories of challenge and triumph, being touched, moved and inspired together I began to discover what I had lost... the power of the feminine.

In retrospect, I see that the culture and time that I was born into knew little of this elusive power, and valued even it less. The Feminine was narrowly defined in relation to being a woman... and then, a woman in relation to men.

In 1995 I was part of the Brahma Kumaris World Spiritual University delegation to the Fourth UN World Conference on Women in Beijing. The Brahma Kumaris (BKs) is a worldwide organization, led by women, elders who are in their eighties and nineties, working in their wisdom and grace for the spiritual renewal of humanity. As part of this mission, the leaders of the BKs commissioned a group of us to develop a follow up to Beijing.

This is when The Four Faces emerged, born of the imagination of an Australian woman named Helen Chapman. Since that time, The Four Faces have been for women. But who knows where they will find themselves and who will wear them in the future?

The VISION – How it Started

In 1993, I had a vision about women. I didn't know what I should do about it. I had never had anything to do with women, apart from being one – and really I didn't ever think of myself as a woman, they were older, more mature than me. I had had few female friends. I had three sisters, but in my eyes they were girls rather than women. So although I trusted the vision, I didn't do anything with it, I didn't take any action about it.

And so it came back again, and again, and again. It haunted me until finally I said to the heavens: "Yes, yes. All right! I'll do something!" What to do I still had no idea, but I wasn't prepared to have this cinemascopic size vision confronting me at random, often distracting, moments in my life.

So a dear friend Silvana helped me. We sat for days locked up in my home writing, rewriting, meditating, offering our humble, sometimes hopeless ideas to a higher, more divine inspiration. Working and waiting and hoping that something would happen... And Women of Spirit was born. We had a small, yet elegant, dialogue with women leaders. After that, on a monthly basis we held Women of Spirit gatherings in the Brahma Kumaris local centre in an inner Sydney suburb. Each month, without promotion beyond a flyer at the centre, somewhere between forty and a hundred women would come to hear stories of inspiration.

I would invite women who travelled the spiritual journey, women from different traditions, paths and religions. Women who had faced and overcome. Women who authentically shared the process of their inner world. Then we would have meditation followed by tea and cake. These meetings were profoundly nourishing.

After that I moved state and the meetings stopped. That's when the Four Faces of Woman began. Women of Spirit re-surfaced a few years ago for me and in 1995 Women of Spirit meetings were adopted in many countries throughout the world and still continue today.

While I trusted the vision, I didn't dedicate myself to it fully. I ran a consulting business for nine years and worked with women 'on the side'. Although in reality, most of my work in the corporate arena was with large organizational transformation, where my clients were mostly women.

So here I am, in 2007, and the vision continues to shape me and my life. Being asked to write this book, launching the beautiful project Leadership & Love, currently based in Chile, a country that elected a woman, Michele Bachelet, as their president.

It all began thirteen years ago with this Vision:

There they were, women clad in different, yet simple white clothing, emerging from all directions, moving independently towards an unseen destination. They moved in complete silence, walking tall in their own power. From where I watched, the qualities of love and humility were deeply etched in their powerful forms.

At some point there was an unseen and silent signal which saw the women turn forming a line as far as the eye could see. They now moved forward as one, focused, side by side. They were still silent, independent, and yet subtly, totally connected. As they moved forward, it was as if I felt the world – all the children, adults, animals and nature – release a deep and grateful sigh of relief.

At this moment, the scene changed and was replaced with the vision of a man.

From what I saw, he represented to me the archetypal economic, political leader of the time – wiry grey hair, rimless glasses, pin-

striped suit, beads of sweat perched on his forehead and brow. He was stressed and appeared to be terribly burdened. He was holding a globe of the world and although heroic, was struggling in his efforts to maintain his grip. Just when he looked as though he couldn't manage any longer, he looked up and saw the women. They moved with such grace. Their humility, love and power meant that they were no threat.

And then I heard the thought in his mind, "Thank God... I don't have to pretend I know what to do anymore."

The vision finished there. But as I said, it didn't leave me alone. It was calling me to do something. To be myself and in so doing, be one of many women becoming our true selves, authentic, beautiful, powerful, loving, tolerant, compassionate, generous, gentle, strong leaders. To be our true selves for ourselves and our world.

THE CONTEXT FOR THE JOURNEY
THROUGH THE FOUR FACES

This time that we are sitting in as a race is perhaps one of the most powerful moments of change in the history of humanity. There are challenges on all fronts – environmental, political, psychological, social, family. There are severe threats to our basic survival.

On the other hand, there is a rapidly growing awareness of these things, as well as the relationship between them and our individual and collective consciousness. There are many of us across the world who are undertaking a commitment to renewal – for ourselves, our lives and our planet.

Indeed we are in an undeniable time of change, and if we choose well and learn the way of energizing, of empowering ourselves, the change can alchemically become a transformation, taking us to a new level of consciousness, awareness, being and living.

With change, sometimes we simply 'move things around'. Like when we move the furniture in our house. Same furniture, same house, but it feels different, better for a time. However when it comes to the journey of the self, when we find after some time that the same pattern re-emerges, it can be disheartening to realize that in fact, nothing really changed below the surface, and we're still not free or at peace or powerful or happy.

The good news is that there is the possibility of real transformation, of being able to transcend old patterns of thinking, of consciousness. If we start with the premise that all that we want, we already are, we just need to trust that and reconnect, then the journey is more about relaxing into being rather than having to become something else. The pressure is turned off, we don't actually need to achieve any more in our lives. Who we are is good enough… if we could just be that more often.

The art simply lies in finding the right methods. Some of these methods, or ways of perceiving, listening and being, are contained in the pages of this book. The rest I am yet to discover for myself. Some are universal and some are no doubt particular to my journey and may not resonate with you at all. Trust yourself. Try. Experiment. Observe. Experiment again. Your world becomes the laboratory, and you the scientist. Your life is the canvas, you are the painter.

The one universal that I would feel confident to guarantee is that there is certainly the presence of the Divine, of God, available in this great time of change to guide each of us.

In these pages you will find some simple thoughts, ways about how to connect energetically to your own divinity as well as the Divine Source. This is a deeply personal connection and doesn't require a religious framework. However, having said this, a religious tradition for some is very important and provides nourishment, community, a sense of belonging as well as a 'container' for the spiritual journey.

Each one's journey is very particular. I have found it most important to find my own true voice – sometimes a mild whisper – to ensure I keep orienting back to my authentic self. My advice to you would be the same advice I give to myself: Learn from all, listen to few, trust myself.

THE ENERGY OF 3

I wanted to take a moment to share a little where the energy of 3 is pertinent to the spiritual journey.

3 Energies of Transformation:

1. Create
2. Sustain
3. Destroy

As soon as you send out a thought or feeling that says anything like "There's something missing", "My life needs to change", "There's got to be more than this", "Who am I?" – you set in motion a very powerful force for change. And the more insistent this thought or feeling, the more powerful the force. You have just activated the *First Energy of Transformation – Creation Energy*.

Once you create an intention, vision, hope, dream, you then have to sustain it through visualization, meditation, aligned action and other methods.

Sustenance is the Second Energy.
Often either the First Energy alone or the First and Second Energies are used, but the *Third Energy is the tricky one: the energy of destroying, letting go of the old, finishing, detaching.*

On the spiritual journey, as the soul awakens to the beauty of its true self, the masks will attempt to survive. After all, that is their raison d'etre. They help us survive when we lose our inner compass, our power, our innate knowing. So it is important to recognize that there will be very critical moments when we are creating that we need to consciously invoke the Third Energy of letting go of the old. If we consciously invoke this energy and use it, the spiritual journey can be marked by struggle creating pain and despair. Naturally this is not optimum.

When you find there is struggle in the soul, you can know it is probably this dilemma.

Simply:

1. Reconnect to your creative impulses, the seed of your dreaming.
2. Put more energy into sustaining the dream, the vision. Visualize. Build strength in your faith. Feel the attainment as a reality. Hold the positive experience, the energy of certainty. Put power into and behind your vision.
3. When there is a stronger feeling around the new, the old will not have as much power over you. You will still need to use the different Powers [1]to let go of the old, but it won't be as great a struggle.

In the chapter on Shakti, there are many tools you will find to help in using these 3 Energies of Transformation.

3 Energies of Time

It is also helpful when reading this book and undertaking the spiritual journey to be conscious of the three aspects of time – using the *past* to understand patterns and insights; divining the *future* and being present in the *now*.

I sometimes think it is a little like walking across a rope bridge that traverses a chasm. I once did an outdoor development exercise on high ropes involving a variety of materials – ropes, chains, boards, tires, ladders and so on – suspended way in the air between trees and poles. I was very aware of what worked and what didn't in terms of getting up and making progress through the course. It was all about consciousness. Thoughts. Focus. Time orientation.

Physically I have what I tend to call a 'full form' these days, and so climbing ten meters into the air and balancing on a rope would appear to be well-nigh impossible or at least a little dangerous. I noticed that if I allowed my thoughts to go anywhere other than being in present in the task, while holding a focused intention of the end point, I would lose my balance.

I observed that if I worried, got distracted, looked back, looked sideways, looked down or became aware of others watching me, I was lost. Simply having my aim and working my conscious awareness in a way that supported me, saw me finish the course without any mishap at all. Everything depends on awareness. That is, understanding that my present thoughts, my presence, creates my future.

As part of moving forward to a better, more empowered future, it is first important to look at where we have come from and where we are. It is not possible to become empowered without first understanding why we are not empowered right now, where and how we lost the power that we vaguely remember having.

It is most helpful to first recognise how conditioning in the past has created the unconscious, powerless identities and patterns that we resort to when we lose our power. It is also useful to know what drives our behaviour, shapes our values, determines our roles, assigns our responsibilities and creates the results that we have in our lives.

So the game is to become clear on the destination, which in many ways is the same for all of us – liberation and love and power and truth and happiness and the return to our own authentic being. How that plays out, how we get there, how we arrive... are unique stories.

Learn to live in the present. Become aware of your thoughts. Choose your thoughts with care, they are a precious resource, your creative power. Random, excessive, unaware thinking wastes energy and usually we're thinking about the past, which means we're resurrecting it in the present and unconsciously creating a future based on what happened yesterday, last week, last year, last decade.

Yet when you hold in your mind and heart the fact that you are

simply returning to your own true nature, there is a kind of famil-
iarity about the journey. The more you relax, tune in, meditate,
connect to your internal and eternal essence, the more clarity and
confidence you get about stepping into an unfolding future.

So if you can almost taste the feeling, smell the experience,
hear the song of your own soul, then you can be sure that the
return is destined, guaranteed, it is just a matter of actively living
it at each moment, consciously choosing the path ahead as if it
were completely unwritten. This is the importance of meditation.

The soul knows the path, it is the mind that will argue the
way. Meditation allows you to be present to your own knowing
that is beyond the limits of a conditioned mind or a controlling
intellect. It enables each one to feel encouraged and affirmed and
to move forward in hope and confidence.

CURIOUS INQUIRIES
– HOW TO USE THIS BOOK

Because this isn't a 'book of truth' per se, rather it is a collection of learnings, thoughts in transition, ideas under experiment, and so on, it is useful to understand this book as a collection of tools, thought starters, mirrors, stimuli, openings, wonderings and curious inquiries.

These next few pages contain invitations only. If it all seems too overwhelming, then simply forget them, just read the book. You may even find that as you read the chapters on the Faces, you need to stop and allow time for processing or integrating. You can either put the book down, coming back to it later, or switch to the stories and reflections in the second part. Part two contains easy reading wisdom of the Four Faces in action, in daily life.

So as you make your way through the book, think about making a few notes when things touch you, jump off the page at you, disturb you, inspire you, ignite you. These notes will be your soul work, specifically identified by you, as important to you at this time.

TOOLS

There are a range of tools that you can adopt and then adapt for your own journey. I suspect you will find that you have to do two lots of work. The first in making the tool 'your own', understanding it within the context of your own world and life experiences. Second, practicing using it, creating the experience of becoming one with the instrument.

Thought Starters

It is now widely known that we have something in the vicinity of 60,000 thoughts every day, and that 95% of those thoughts are the same ones we had yesterday! So in order to overcome the powerful patterns of a lifetime, we really need to use our thinking to create better thoughts... and ideally, after some time, fewer, more effective thoughts. Because thoughts are our creative energy and our creation starters, it is useful to use our intellects to think in new ways if we want to create new patterns and a different, more enhanced future life.

As you read, it could be helpful to keep a notebook with you, to jot down any ideas that strike you – either in a positive, a curious or even a negative, reactive way. Then throughout your day, think through these ideas. Make your intellect work *for* you, not *against* you. If I have a negative reaction against something, or start to criticise, I always find it helpful for my learning, to ask: "If this were true, how might I understand it differently?" I don't always end up agreeing with the proposition, however to ask this question frees me from fixed and rigid, defensive belief patterns and allows me to go somewhere new and fresh in my understanding.

Mapping

In a similar way, if one of the ideas makes you feel a loss of self-esteem, it is important to know that there is nothing in this book intended to do that. Everything here is written as a support for seeing clearly and moving beyond limiting patterns. So if an old pattern is sabotaging you, create a small space in your day – ten minutes will probably do – and make a mind map[2].

Or you can look in the chapter on The New Intelligences and use the HOW I FEEL matrix if that appeals to you more. Either the matrix or the mapping will do a number of things.

First, it detaches you from your mind. This is very, very useful.

Second, it helps you get perspective on the neurological patterns or 'clusters' that collect around your reaction. You can start to see that they're not 'real' as such, they're just recurring patterns that your mind does out of habit.

Third, you can sometimes see where the seed of the pattern began, and sometimes just seeing that, can help dissolve it.

On the other hand, if you ignore or suppress or push away a reaction, you may have lost an opportunity to undo something that is not serving you and is even perhaps sabotaging you.

Mirrors

Which brings me to mirrors. Why is it that a situation can evoke different reactions from different people? The scene in and of itself can be relatively innocuous, however the reaction that it triggers can be very insightful.

So throughout this book, if you find yourself responding or reacting in certain ways, remember that it is not me or the book, your reaction belongs to you… it is part of your story, it is an opportunity for you to discover something about you. And when you take on this responsibility, you take back your power. You no longer allow someone or something to be responsible for how you feel.

I don't mean to say that I'm not responsible. I feel very responsible and have taken great care and a lot of time to finally pen these pages. However, it goes against the ethos of this book for you to blame me or the book or the stories of the women in its pages, for your feelings. Blame is a process of disempowering oneself. It gives another the power to define us.

Owning our feelings is a place of power, even if those feelings feel unbearable at times. Only by owning feelings and not suppressing or avoiding feeling them, can we hope to take charge of our lives, become masters of our own destiny.

Sometimes it is true that I don't feel strong enough to handle a situation or own a feeling. The spiritual journey is a process where I accumulate strength, energy and wisdom through meditation and experience to be able to handle whatever comes. As I use this accumulated energy, I realise that I do have the power to be in charge, and in turn, this gives me more confidence, more strength.

So this book may be a mirror, and certainly all relationships provide wonderful mirrors. I remember when I first understood this notion it was pure liberation.

Sometimes seeing one's inner world is slippery business and of course it is much easier to diagnose the problems of others than it is to recognise the subtleties of one's own challenges. However, mirrors can be profoundly helpful in this. Try this:

When someone annoys me, drives me crazy, ask what attitude or behaviour are they demonstrating that is a mirror of something within me that I wouldn't otherwise see?

When someone inspires me, what are they showing me about myself that I wouldn't otherwise own?

When something touches me, haunts me, angers me, affronts me, what am I being shown about my inner world that is a chance to be more in charge of my life?

Pure liberation. Utterly free. Totally responsible. Extremely empowering.

It is unlikely that any of us can change another, no matter how we might try, so until we own and transform our 'stuff', we will always be triggered, if not by that individual or situations, by someone or something else that is almost identical. That means that we are controlled by external circumstances, our lives are not our own.

Understanding that people and situations are mirrors, that they are helpful, is a powerful key to becoming masterful on this journey. Blame keeps us stuck. Taking responsibility in a non-judgemental, yet honest and kind way gets us in motion.

Mirrors are gifts. The interesting thing is, that when we've accepted the gift in a particular mirror, when we've opened it and embraced it and used the gift for learning and transformation, the image in the mirror vanishes, the triggers disappear. The person or the situation remains, but you will notice a miracle... that you no longer have the reaction that you once had. And you hardly notice the behaviour that used to infuriate you.

Stimuli

In addition to the stimulus of thought starters and mirrors, you will notice that ideas that capture your attention in this book will show up in your external environment. Whatever you focus your attention on, your subconscious and your higher self will scan the environment for other ideas, situations, people, opportunities that align to your focus.

So it is helpful to consciously choose an idea or concept or practice that you can use to stimulate alignment in your external environment.

An example is that when I was reading my friend Stephanie Dowrick's latest book *Choosing Happiness*, I took the point that 'love can be the context of life'. Not just being in love with one person, or even loving life, but Love as a way of life, a filter through which to see everything, to contain the living experience.

Holding this thought as a stimulus, I began to see how many things and people and situations I didn't appreciate and how appreciating them made me love them and that it was easy to appreciate if I simply focused. And as appreciation gave me back the experience of loving, it also connected me to the Love that I am, expanding myself, connecting me to all, a sense of oneness. No neediness, no separation.

My sister gave me a book which in one of my many house moves, I somehow misplaced so I never got to read it. However, the proposition on the front of the book changed my life. I can't remember the title of the book (although it had the word 'dance' in it), nor can I recall the author and yet this one proposition gave a new clarity to the way I do this journey, the way I understand myself and others. So thank you whoever you are! And it was just a few words.

What if the question was not, why do I so infrequently be the person I want to be, but rather why do I so infrequently want to be the person I am?

Thinking about this, being stimulated by this thought, is when I realised that who I am is more than enough, if I could just be that more often. This thought will no doubt be repeated often in this book, as it has become the foundation for my understanding of the spiritual journey.

As I allowed this stimulus to seep into my awareness, a whole new set of people and conversations emerged for me, re-affirming this inherent wisdom.

So think about using the ideas in this book as stimuli for your own active process of learning and scanning for learning.

Openings, Wonderings and Curious Inquiries

If something doesn't makes sense, if you don't agree with something. If you have an intuitive feeling that a story, an idea or a paragraph has a message or insight for you... please don't ignore the feeling. This book is your work in progress. The invitation is to recognise when it is opening up an opportunity for you to explore you. The offer is to diagnose your resistance or resonance and let them take you somewhere deeper within yourself. The proposition is to let yourself become curious about yourself and about possibilities and about the nature of life and living and the spiritual journey which is a wondrous inquiry in itself.

As you open this book, let it open you to yourself in a new way, sometimes in a challenging way, yet always in a beautiful way. Really, this is it is only purpose and perhaps indeed the purpose of this life, to 'Know thyself'.

Intention

Now that you have a sense of what is contained in terms of process in this book, I suggest that before beginning to read, you make a note about what you would personally like to gain from engaging with this book. As you know, in the many thousands of words on these pages, each reader will find what is most relevant for them, interpret it, and connect with it. You can do this on automatic pilot, scanning the pages based on past, unconscious or unrevised patterns, or you could take this chance to update. More will definitely be gained if your journey through this book is proactive.

Where are you at now?

What are the questions that you are asking now in your life?

What's important, relevant, interesting, challenging now?

What are you looking for, hoping for, creating now, for which you would welcome some added input?

Intention is different from traditional goal setting. Intention allows for you to work in partnership with God, with the *universe of right order*, with the magic of the spiritual journey. It says: 'Set an intention that is specific and yet open. Allow for more to enter your world than you could personally create and then stay awake because there will be signals and situations that show up that are completely aligned to your intention'.

Many years ago, I wanted to buy a new car, well new for me. I didn't know what kind of car I wanted but a friend said, "Talk to

Doug, he'll be able to help you." And help me he did. Over a cup of tea, and after an expansive list of questions, Doug finally let out a satisfied "Aha, that's it." I waited in anticipation. "What you want is a Peugeot 505."

"Do I? Great!" Followed by the thought... 'What's a Peugeot 505?' I'd never even heard of Peugeot leave aside a Peugeot 505. But not to worry, Doug had not finished his role of new car guide. Off we went to the used car dealer for Peugeot just twenty minutes from home.

I have to admit to feeling quite excited at the prospect of a French car. I thought it rather exotic, definitely unique and although secondhand, it would have a certain something about it.

As we drove in to the yard, Doug pointed out two samples of said 505. He was right. This was the car for me. We settled almost immediately on the silver one with the black leather interior and sunroof. (As a vegetarian, I still feel uncomfortable with the fact that I sat on dead cow for so long!)

Anyway, the point of the story is that, after Doug checked it thoroughly and gave it the thumbs up, I put a deposit on the car. I soon would have my own special, very unique, French automobile. As we drove the twenty minutes back home, I swear that I saw at least 30 Peugeot 505s on the road. For a moment my special, unique ego was devastated. How could this be? I had never seen one before and now I'm seeing hundreds! And that's the point.

There are an infinite number of pieces of information floating around in our world. We don't have the capacity to absorb or process all of it, not even ten percent of it. So unless we set a new intention, a new focus on a regular basis, or update our higher level focus, realign to it, we won't see a lot of what is available to us. However, by clarifying intentions, we open up to a whole world that is there but that we haven't yet seen.

What we focus on is what we perceive. Then we become active participants in our lives, weaving throughout our days capturing the magic.

The invitation is to set your intention for engaging with this book in the same way. Allow yourself to scan and interpret according to where you are at right now in your journey, but keeping in mind where you hope to be, what your dream is for your future. It may be that in a year or two, you redefine, re-clarify and enter the book in a different and new space. You will then reap very different learning. This puts you in charge of this journey. This makes you the one with the power to capture, create and change.

The Soul's Journey

The Four Faces are not religious in nature or form, they are however very much the soul's journey. They certainly help us to understand institutionalized religion – it is attraction for some, it is repulsion for others – but I believe they exist to be understood by anyone wanting to find answers to the age old questions:

Who am I?
Who or what is God – if there is indeed a God?
What does it all mean?

If any or all of these questions sit as part of your unresolved self, then you will certainly find The Four Faces of enormous value.

The journey into and through the Faces is both gentle and powerful. They will undo your perception of yourself and your world, but they will do so with great reverence for your sensitivity and inherent beauty. They hold within them the unraveling of your own knowing, your personal spirituality, your individual path, your own unique purpose for being.

The Four Faces provide us with a way of seeing ourselves more clearly, of how we can either limit or liberate ourselves through our thinking, perception and attitudes. They offer us a mirror in which to see that which undermines our happiness. They reflect our inherent beauty and strength, giving us the courage to believe that we are important, that we have something of real value to contribute – no matter how seemingly small or apparently grand. In relation to purpose, size doesn't count at all. Rather it is our willingness and the quality of our generosity that matters.

In this awakened state of awareness, aligned to our living purpose, we might then change, dissolve, destroy, let go of and finish, old attitudes and behaviours that we have never questioned before. Indeed, if awake to our own transformative power, would we choose to perpetuate generations of tradition that we might understand to be inherently unjust? Would we use different, more subtle powers to transform wrong to right rather than using violence against violence? Would we learn how to allow ourselves to be as powerful as mythology tells us that the energy of the feminine is? Would we? Could we? Might we? Is it possible?

This book and the available 4Faces retreats and workshops run by the Brahma Kumaris throughout the world – see www.bkwsu.org – are designed specifically to support women in moving forward consciously in a way that is positive and trans-formational for themselves, their families and their world.

There are many women who facilitate this program and carry nuances, experiences and understanding about the faces that I'm not privy to. And of course the participants, the many thousands of magnificent women who have challenged, questioned, jumped in and trusted when they weren't sure, who shared and dreamed, all helping to unlock the secrets behind each of the Faces. No doubt you too will discover new and refined insights as you welcome The Four Faces into your life.

So this is my version, out of my experience, my daily experiments and my memory. As insightful and as limited as it might be … it is here.

Please accept it with love.

The Eternal Face

Where we begin and where we're heading.

It carries the truth of our innate innocence and authentic power.

It holds safe, our ability to wonder and delivers us our inherent beauty, our unique gifts and a resonant sense of infinite knowing.

It is our essential being... it is Essence.

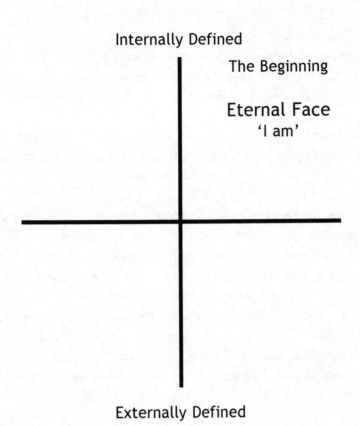

THE ETERNAL FACE

'I AM'

*When the person is first alive, using body and mind, discovering
relationships and nature, its outlook is so new and pure; it lives under
a sense of natural wonder...
I can get in touch with this part of my self; I can actively awaken
that memory...
In my present busy life, I can still rest in the power that arises from
remembering innocence, purity and the beauty coming from newness...*
Valeriane Bernard

The Eternal Face is both the beginning of our journey and it is the
completion point. This is the state of *I am* – no questions, doubts,
confusion, duality, no wondering, just 'is-ness' and 'being'. Self-
respect, confidence, no need to prove anything to anyone, 100%
pure 'me energy' – not mixed with anyone or anything else.

No shadows, no grey, no uncertainty. Utter clarity and
centredness.

Surely this face only appears in moments? Glimpses of it that
last seconds, maybe days if we're not too busy, too engrossed in
activities and demands and responsibilities?

That depends. Depends on if we can remember the purity of
certainty, the clarity of rest. If we can – and the soul definitely can
– then we will spend our entire lives in the art of reconnecting
with our own truth.

The heartening news is that the Eternal Face is always with us.
It is immortal and so can never be destroyed although it can
certainly be diminished in presence. Because it is truth and
because truth is indestructible, who we are is also indestructible,
eternal. However we send this face away, put it to sleep, tell it
we're not interested, we don't trust it, doubt its beauty and its
power. We stop believing in the wonder of this sacred self, we

start believing in the formulas of others. But once we tap back into our own innate source, we find that there is a veritable treasure store of precious jewels and tools for living.

The Eternal Face carries the secrets of manifestation... pure and easy manifestation, etched clearly and keenly in the contours of its invisible self. Our original nature is that of creative being, of being able to think and move directly into form.

This is the original art of living before we began to doubt ourselves and listen to others. This was the way of things and it is why somewhere in our subconscious, we believe that we ought to be able to do much, much more and be much, much more fulfilled than we are.

Simply because it exists as a strong memory, a blueprint, a spiritual DNA within the soul, we can know that the way of things is flow and pure order. That creative potential is meant to manifest. That we are beings of joy and that life was and is somehow meant to be more magical than mundane.

But how? It is true, there's no point in reawakening the memory and the hope that we ought to be able to live like this, be like this and do like this, if we can't recapture the method, the way, the Tao of it all. That would be cruel. And depressing. So yes, of course there is a how. Well many hows, with key life themes, simple practices that need to be accompanied by an attitude of experimentation, a gentle yet firm commitment to relearning, remembering and re-establishing the way. Held safe in the virtue of patience, because it takes a lifetime.

So sit back, relax. This book is designed absolutely to offer you practical insights and simple methods to reconnect with the natural sacredness of your Eternal Face.

Setting Your Intention

If you haven't already set your intention (which can encompass a range of hopes, dreams, feeling, thoughts as a focus) as outlined in How to Use this Book, may I suggest that you do that now before going any further? I guarantee that you'll find it enormously helpful.

Uncovering the Hidden Jewel

The Eternal Face is about awareness, a way of seeing and a way of being. If we look at new little souls, just arrived, there is an incredible innocence, an outrageous power that they possess to influence even the crustiest adult. When I talk about babies, I don't mean the ones that look about 300 years old – you know the ones that you just know have been around before. I mean the brand new, squeaky clean, fresh ones who are here for the first time. When they get to that age of really connecting with you, they simply have the power to transform. I have watched at airports, in shopping centres and in cinemas the way in which adults can have their demeanours turned about by the innocence of children. Their natural curiosity, their power of truth, their openness and straightforward nature is sheer delight to us older souls who have bought into convention, who have already had the wings of our spirits clipped.

The same phenomenon occurs with newly born animals. Often they're just way too cute! Why? They are not self-conscious in anyway, they haven't yet learned any protective mechanisms to inhibit their naturalness.

One sunny weekday in Melbourne, Australia, where I was living, I caught a tram to the city just ten minutes from my home. The tram was easier than driving and parking in the city, and it always offered me a window through which to see the wonder of humanity. On this day, a group of young schoolboys was causing disturbance. They were shouting, running up and down the crowded tram and generally making it a very uncomfortable ride. A couple of people had ventured to ask them to manage themselves better, but to no avail. And then the most wonderful thing happened. An older woman in her seventies got on the tram and she had with her a tiny puppy. It was a typical puppy – soft, fluffy, white and outrageously cute, even for those not particularly fond of dogs. Within about ten seconds, the boys had stopped their overzealous play and were oooohing and aaaaahing over the puppy. The innocence was so powerful, it pulled from them their own innocence. They helped the woman off the tram a few stops on, and all sat down quietly until it was their stop to get off, which they did with a kind of natural respect for the rest of us on the tram. After they got off, the passengers who were left all looked at each other amazed. Really, quite shocked at such a starkly transformed scene.

This innocence is so powerful because it mirrors for us the original state of our own selves. Coming face to face with the natural sacredness, the unadorned spirit, the authentic being, we are consciously or even unconsciously reminded and even reconnected to the feeling of our own essence, our own truth. It is a presence, a state of being in *now* that awakens us to something deep within ourselves.

When we can be present, not thinking about, or worrying about the future, not regretting, reminiscing or lamenting the past, but totally present in the Now, then we can start to tune into the frequency of the energy of the Eternal Face.

Plato said that if you can find your way onto the knife-edge of Now, you will glimpse eternity.

Given that I don't have my body for more than a hundred years, then eternity must be something subtle, not to be glimpsed with the physical eyes. This is where the term 'third eye' comes in, or divine vision.

The more that we connect with the subtle qualities of the soul or self, the more we start to become aware of, and see, the subtle world of thought and energy. When we start to 'see' this invisible world, to recognise that these states of being are what we resonate with, long for, seek, then we are on our way to experiencing states like love, peace, bliss, power, truth, contentment, joy more often in our everyday lives. We are on our return to the Eternal Face.

It's not like we haven't tried. Of course we have. Every moment of every day, in every act we undertake, we are seeking to find our way back to our Eternal Face, our essence.

The songs that we love, the movies we watch, the stories that stay with us, the sunsets we delight in, the forests that soothe us, the people who make us laugh, who comfort us or make us feel special, the churches, temples, mosques, and other places of worship that we visit, the make-up we wear, the new shoes we buy, the meals we make... all these are sincere but often lacklustre attempts to recover the tenderness of our original state.

It may not seem that this is so, but if we were to examine each action we undertake in our lives, looking deeply we would definitely find that the driver, the underlying and often unconscious motivation, is to experience either one or more of these original qualities.

There's an exercise in the workshop we do with the Four Faces, where we look to find our deepest motivations behind action. You choose three mundane actions that you perform in your life, and then start to dig. With a partner (or on your own) you start searching for what lies beneath the surface tasks. The results can seem extraordinary... and yet not.

Sometimes grocery shopping is about experiencing peace. As ridiculous as this might sound, especially if you dislike grocery shopping, read the following experience from Rose in Nairobi and see if it makes sense.

1. Why do I go shopping?
2. To fill the cupboard.
3. When the cupboard is full what does that do?
4. It makes everyone in the house happy.
5. When everyone else is happy what does that do for me?
6. I feel relieved.
7. When I feel relieved, what does that make me feel?
8. At peace.

Now you might challenge that this is not an ideal way to get peace, and you'd probably be right. This is not the point of the exercise, though. This exercise is simply designed to help us identify what exists underneath each action no matter how mundane or how grand, or even negative.

Other insights through this exercise have been:

I drive in the traffic to find peace.
I eat to experience love.
I work to feel content.
I cook to feel happy.
I run to feel content.
I clean the toilet to be happy.
I get angry at my son to feel at peace.
I control in order to feel safe.
I exclude in order to feel powerful.

The negative activities like 'arguing with my husband' can reap similar results. Even if you are reluctant to admit it, if you follow the process, the questioning leads you to something more noble, more aligned to the original qualities of the human soul: the qualities of purity, power, peace, happiness, love or truth.

The way in which they go about arriving at these qualities will have unfortunate consequences and the attainment of the experience will no doubt be short-lived, however, we are almost programmed to return to the Eternal Face, even if we're doing it at a deeply subconscious level.

Advertising agencies all over the world know that this is human nature. They know absolutely that we are consistently drawn to return to our core values, our original essence, our eternal qualities. Now it is unlikely that they would frame it in those terms, however they do know that every human being on this planet seeks love, peace, happiness, freedom, truth, power and bliss.

Next time you pass a billboard read what's written there:

In Australia you can buy love for just $24,990 (a car).
Another car – you don't drive it, you date it!
A small bottle of green coloured water with bubbles and sugar
will give you freedom.
A particular fashion label offers you 'cool' – the promise of
acceptance and self esteem for a few hundred dollars.
Of course a tropical island holiday will offer you peace of
mind, freedom, potentially love, probably bliss and definitely
happiness.
Computers give you power.
And the list goes on.

And we buy into the advertising sales pitch because we are
subconsciously driven to reconnect with our essential selves
which is being marketed as an ideal version of ourself. We pay
our money to close the gap between our idealized selves and our
actual selves, and we may or may not get a hit of what we were
seeking, but if we do, like any drug that promises a high, it
doesn't seem to last very long.

When we start to really uncover the Eternal Face there is an
enormous sense of relief. Slowly it becomes apparent that so
many of the things we do are unnecessary when we know how to
fulfil our deepest desires through connecting to the Eternal Face,
the essence of being, and practicing simple techniques and
awareness.

All over the world, women are awakening to themselves, to
their real desires, to their true hopes and dreams. And not surprisingly, these women are discovering that the culture of accumu-
lation and materialism has not been satisfying them for a long
time. We have been deluded. It has all been illusion.

It is one thing to wake up and say this isn't working for me, but
it is another thing altogether to know what to do about it.

The Eternal Face is the reality that lives behind the longing, the memory. The first step in reclaiming it is to acknowledge its existence.

If I search for love, I must know love.
If I hunger for peace, I must have felt peace before.
If I want joy, then joy must have been part of my world at some point.
If I can imagine purity of life, then I must intrinsically resonate with purity.
If being authentic is important to me, then it makes sense that truth is core to my very nature.

We have had the habit for a long, long time of looking outwards, of asking others the way. The Four Faces is a turning within. The Eternal Face is available to each one of us – absolutely – it does however require a commitment to resuscitate it.

The Eternal Face has been buried for a long time for most of us. It is a miracle even that it still survives. But truth can never be killed, spirit never dies and the Eternal Face is pure spirit.

Returning to the Eternal Face as a full time way of life rather than simply glimpses of its beauty, is a commitment, an undertaking which is given strength and courage by a deep yearning within the soul. To know that there are millions of women and men the world over beginning and resuming the way of the soul also gives solace to the traveller. The process is a life long journey. It is adventuresome, beautiful and filled with magic.

The process of coming home to the Eternal Face is guided by the Face of the Shakti, our highest self and knowing. This is the Face that takes the role of the wise one, the protector of the essence, the observer and the alchemist. Shakti rescues us from illusion in the Traditional and Modern Faces, and she breathes life and strength back into the soul.

She is the wisest part of ourselves and she is the Fourth Face.

Her way is comprised of the following:

Knowing
Connecting
Being
Sharing

Shakti takes us to ourselves. She has powers, she has perspective and she is always available. This is the face within each of us, whose time is Now. Shakti is the face that aligns us to the practice of remembering and reconnecting with who we really are.

Knowing Practice

The following are suggestions on how to bring the knowing about the Eternal Face into reality. They are simple practices that truly make the world of difference.

Affirmations repeated throughout the day:

'At my essence, I am pure. I am light. I am love.'
'At my essence, I am powerful and peaceful.'

See if you can observe your feelings after you successfully complete tasks, activities, interactions. Notice the 'pay off', or underlying motivation.

Become aware of the energy that is alive inside your body, a kind of tingling sensation. Immerse yourself in this awareness as often as possible.

This energy is the extended life force of the soul in the physical form. The soul, essence, consciousness, sits behind the forehead, using the wondrous faculty of the brain for working the body and taking action in the world. We extend our life force throughout the body giving energy to all it is parts.

Connection Practice
Practice being 'present', in the Now.
There are a range of ways to do this including:

- Listening... to another, to your breathing, to the world, just listening
- Drawing, colouring, painting, sculpting, dancing...artistic expression *without* judgement...just being *in* the expression
- Being 'mindful' as the Buddhist term goes... consciously aware of all the actions you do, even the smallest of actions
- Imagine yourself as a tiny sparkling star, living behind the centre of the forehead, shining – this gives you a great visual metaphor and helps us to let go of the fragile, even false identities with which we constantly associate.

When you become aware of the inner energetic body, and the originating source of that energy as the self, it is easy then to experience this as your 'light body'.

The more you sense this inner energy as a body of light, the more easily you are able to disconnect from the constructs of the ego and reconnect to the subtleties of your true self.

Meditation
One of the best ways to connect, and to strengthen your capacity to be connected more often to your own essence, is meditation. There are many kinds of meditation and you can access these easily through the Internet, bookshops, classes.

I haven't tried them all, but the one I love is Raja Yoga meditation because it is a silent form, and you can do it with your eyes open or closed. This means you can do it anywhere, at almost anytime. It is just a matter of shifting your awareness and using your thinking capacity in a conscious and a more inspired, helpful way.

Essentially Raja Yoga (Raja means king / sovereign / ma

Yoga is connection), is the practice of connecting with and resting in the subtle energy that is you, the soul.

You can use the image of the star, any of the practices above, or even thoughts/words to guide the mind to an experience of the self, your consciousness/awareness *before* we were born into a body.

The more we are able to reconnect with the 'seed' of who we are prior to any conditioning, the easier it is hold the distinction and feeling when in everyday action. Then it is just a matter or remembering that feeling.

The following is a very simple visualization. If you don't find it easy to visualize in meditations, that's okay, just have a sense of what is suggested to see.

Beings of Light Meditation

So imagine yourself, your thinking feeling self, that is your awareness, the one who watches, who observes, who notices the thoughts and feelings, travelling to the sky beyond the sky.

This sky is a subtle dimension of golden red light, deeply silent and completely still. Just allow yourself to tune into the feeling here, ask yourself what would the frequency of this place, this dimension of silent, golden, warm light be like.

As you rest here, you become aware of tiny sparks of pure consciousness, beings of light, naturally emanating gentle, powerful light. They are completely stable, absolutely secure.

See if you can feel the atmosphere of total safety and complete security. Watch or sense how they are absolutely protected.

In this dimension, these beings of light are gently held in power and in love. They are with the Source, the Supreme who, just like them is a et is a utterly radiant fountain of pure love.

ch or sense these beings, become aware if you can, how ted in a very natural way to the Supreme, to this source. ine into one of these souls and feel the love that is filling source. Do that now. Feel the energy that is coming to

this being of light from the source of light. Pure love. Feel the frequency
of this pure energy. Tune into the feeling of security. Enjoy this feeling
for a few minutes.

Now gently find yourself bringing your awareness back to the
physical – your body and the room bringing with you the feelings you
connected with in this meditation.

Tuning into the Essence Meditation

This meditation uses a familiar metaphor to take you from the physical
to the subtle. Remember that connection with your Eternal Face is about
becoming more aligned to pure, subtle feelings than to an identity that
is associated with the body, it is roles and relationships. It is about
tuning into the essence.

So just sit comfortably and imagine that we are going to visit the
'house of the self'.

Find yourself standing in front of a beautiful gate. As you stand
there, you feel a little excitement at the thought of coming 'home' to
yourself. But you also feel patient, knowing that this is a gentle process
and will come in it is own time.

Now you are feeling the cool metal of the key in your hand, you look
down and see your feet. Remember that this is your key, your gate, your
home. Reaching out, you put the key in the lock and it opens effortlessly.
As you step through to the path that leads to the very lovely home, you
become aware of the warmth of the sun on your skin and the gentle
breeze caressing your hair. You even hear the sound of your footsteps on
the path and feel the texture of the path under your feet.

Arriving at the door, you pause. Here you have the opportunity to
leave any 'baggage' that might get in the way of this journey. You will
pass by here on the way out and so can collect it then if you want to. So
leave whatever you want to leave now.

When that is done, you will start to move toward the place, the space
that is the Eternal Face. It may be a room inside the house, or it may be
a special place in the gardens or grounds. Don't think, just go there
now.

Wherever you go will be very beautiful, very comfortable and you will feel totally at home. If by chance you feel anything other than lovely and comfortable, you have detoured and gone to the wrong place, simply turn around and go to the right place. Easily and naturally.

Finding yourself there now, allow yourself to become very, very comfortable. Feel how it feels to be 'home'. The more that you allow yourself to 'rest in this place', the more you find you are this place. A perfect fit.

...Imagine you can simply settle in, nuzzle down, soak up the atmosphere of this place

...Simply sink in and let yourself be at one.

... Allow yourself to stay here for a few minutes enjoying the subtle feelings of this space.

After some time...

Now gently, start to gather your awareness, bringing with you to the front door of the house, the subtle feelings and energies that you connected with in this place. These are yours to bring with you into the outer world.

Gather any baggage you are not ready to leave behind and make your way up the path, locking the gate behind you.

How to Reflect on the Practice

Affirm what you did accomplish, it makes the next time more enticing, gives you more confidence to have a go, and you leave the practice with a positive result. It is much better to go off into the day feeling good about yourself. Remember too, that what you focus on is what you see, and what you see is where you direct your energy. So it makes sense to give life to the small accomplishments or moments of experience rather than the minutes of distraction or mindless thinking or drowsiness. Focus on what you want to create more of in your life. This gives you the strength, the courage and the enthusiasm to address the areas that need developing.

Make a few notes in your journal. For example, you might note that you managed to stay alert the whole time, you didn't fall asleep. Or if you didn't seem to see anything, notice that you definitely felt peaceful. Or even if your thoughts were going in different directions, you did somehow manage to go to that place. Or you may notice that you left your baggage at the door and didn't want to collect it on the way out. Or the breeze in your hair before you fell asleep.

Advanced Practice

Go to your place as in the previous practice, and this time, allow the space to open up and invite God, the Source, the Divine into your space.

Allow the light of the Supreme to comfort you, to fill you, to reflect to you your own divinity.

Internally Defined

The Beginning

Eternal Face
'I am'

Traditional Face
'I am who you say
I am'

Externally Defined

The Traditional Face

It tries to contain essence, to protect it. It sets up rules, boundaries, which endeavour to secure.

Good intent becomes control and soon our world is full of 'no'.

In its attempt to maintain order, safety, harmony, it diminishes our world and limits our capacity to experience the wonder and joy of being.

As our world shrinks, we shrink. Labels and roles become the new identity.

THE TRADITIONAL FACE

"I AM WHO YOU SAY I AM"

At some point in time arises socialization; for fear of some unseen or
visible danger, and complex realities Woman has a new role to play…
Beautiful child bearer, healer, earth, guardian of family, of children …
She becomes encircled by a law and a system of protection.
From protection to fear, from fear to protection, fear of sorrow, the
birth of evil is declared…
From encircled to jailed the step is very small…
And the world is full of women who were hurt and damaged in the
name of laws, visible ones… Stoned to death… invisible ones … guilt
and inadequacy creeping in like snakes in the dark of loneliness….
Invisible to the self even.
I am affected and I am 'naturally' encircling my self in laws, I feel
security in mighty rules, I feel insecure without them, I don't always
understand nor perceive this in my own life.
Valeriane Bernard

When we lose ourselves, becoming rather than playing our beautiful roles of mother, partner, lover, friend, home maker, healer, teacher and wisdom keeper, these roles then shape shift into narrow traps that confine our spirit and shrink our expression.

Once this happens, we disconnect from our innate knowing, our natural wisdom and begin to trust more in others than ourselves. We seek guidance from experts, sublimating our inherent knowing. Learning is one thing, but deference is altogether something else. How many women have inherently known something was not right with their children or their own bodies, and yet allowed a medical expert tell them differently only to discover they were right later, and sometimes too late. Yet, when connected to our Eternal beingness, we are intuitively wise and we trust our wisdom. We know how to live, how to parent, how to love and how to heal. We don't need others to tell us. We may partner with an expert, but it is a partnership. However, when we lose our connection with our eternal nature, the subtle story of our own soul's energy, we lose our source of power, and we give the power to others to define us.

Losing this connection with ourselves, we lose our natural connection with others and with our natural environment. We become separate and therefore not responsible. From separation, isolation also emerges as a normal, acceptable, although often lonely state. And yet because the nature of being human is to be connected, to experience 'oneness', to feel whole and at peace, when we lose this we do whatever we can to return to that feelings. Belonging, acceptance and finding peace become important and are significant motivations of the Traditional Face. We trade parts of ourselves to keep the peace, to be accepted, to belong. We conform so that there is harmony, oneness. However we need to suppress underlying dissatisfaction to achieve these states. Ultimately the superficiality it is not satisfying to the soul - we are still separate and we are vulnerable.

Then our deepest drive kicks in and we look for ways to remain safe. We look to be with those who look like us, sound like us, seem like us - those who reflect 'us back to us' so that we don't feel lost, so that we feel secure. We set up boundaries, borders and frameworks to keep the feeling of unity, of oneness, to keep the danger of difference away, a danger that reminds us that we are no longer whole, that we are not secure, that we fractured.

In the Traditional Face consciousness, danger can be represented by anything that is a 'perceived threat' to our physical, emotional, psychological or spiritual security. Therefore we feel most safe with those who are most like us. Anyone who is different (men/women, white/black, masters/slaves, conservatives/creatives and so on), anyone whom we don't understand or doesn't understand us, threatens our sense of security at some level and as such, somehow becomes the 'enemy'.

A young friend told me that he and his Chilean brother caught a plane from Jakarta just after the Bali bombing. My friend's brother was around twenty years old, dark and had a full beard. As these young men boarded the plane, a few North American passengers started to panic, eventually managing to disembark. The young man in question is one of the most peace loving, kind, young people you could hope to meet, yet his appearance was judged as malevolent due to the current socio/political circumstances.

This is what we do as human beings when we lose our identity and take on the 'form' as 'who we are'. What we don't understand because of the many differences related to body, we exclude. We label ourselves and others in order to feel good about ourselves. We label others to feel in control, to feel safe. These labels are interpretative and superficial but we adopt them and assign them as if they carried the stamp of God's own Truth.

Then we make decisions based on these interpretations. The witch hunts of the Middle Ages are a prime example. The extermination of the Jews during World War II is another, the hunt for terrorists, school yard ostracising because of culture, physical appearance, sporting ability, religion, intelligence, artistic preferences, sexual orientation and more, are all examples of the Traditional Face in action.

So how are traditions formed? Where do the rules begin? How do we actually learn what we can and cannot, should and should not do or be? Not all of the prevailing conditions are written. Very few of them are laws. So how do they become reality?

Some of these boundaries are selfish needs on behalf of others while many are born from care and with our protection, with benefit in mind. Don't go near the edge you might fall and hurt yourself, or worse still, die. Don't talk to strangers, it is dangerous, you might get raped, kidnapped or killed. Do well at school so you can succeed (and maybe also you can make your parents or teachers proud and look good.) Don't be friends with people from other races or religions or cultural backgrounds because you never know what influence they may have on you or your beliefs. More subtle than that. If you want to belong here, you must look like 'this', sound like 'that', know 'him' or 'her'. If you want to survive and become 'someone', you need to think like us, dress like us, invest like us, act like us. Labels like nice girl, clever girl, dutiful wife, well-behaved daughter are all progeny of the Traditional Face.

This Face needs to belong, to be accepted, to be loved, to be approved, to be affirmed. These are all basic human, spiritual needs and so to fulfil our needs, we adopt the labels, become the roles, be who we need to be, do what we need to do. When we have forgotten who we are, we also forget that we are naturally connected and therefore we inherently belong to all. We also lose the knowing that we are love, loved and loving.

When we forget who we are, that we are eternal, energy, powerful, loving and whole, we subconsciously endeavour to emulate these states through external constructed identities...and the Ego is born. The ego becomes our way of moving in the world, of surviving.

Unfortunately the ego is fragile and can be shattered at any moment – a passing insult, an exclusion, rejection, criticism, oversight, comparison, job loss, divorce, death, disability. Therefore the ego constantly encounters the underlying anxiety of potential loss, of imminent demise and so further protective, defensive energy is needed. Constructed lives absorb vast personal energy without any final guarantees of safe passage.

The Role of Mother
One of the more subtly deceptive ego identities is that of mother. Because the nature of this role is so intimate – emotionally, psychologically and physically – it is near to impossible for women who are mothers not to lose themselves in and attach

themselves to that role. For many, the almost complete subsumption into the role identity of Mother means that they *exist* only in relation to children, mostly theirs but it can be other children also. The Mother then *needs* the children in order to survive, to be valid, to *be*. The children become the means for survival, their energy, a source of power for the mother.

Kahlil Gibran's beautiful poem gives insight into this beautiful, important yet challenging role.

> *Your children are not your children.*
> *They are the sons and daughters of Life's longing for itself.*
> *They come through you but not from you,*
> *And though they are with you yet they belong not to you.*
> *You may give them your love but not your thoughts, for they have*
>   *their own thoughts.*
> *You may house their bodies but not their souls,*
> *For their souls dwell in the house of tomorrow,*
> *Which you cannot visit, not even in your dreams.*
> *You may strive to be like them, but seek not to make them like you.*
> *For life goes not backward nor tarries with yesterday.*
> *You are the bows from which your children as living arrows are*
>   *sent forth.*
> *The Archer sees the mark upon the path of the infinite, and He*
>   *bends you with His might that his arrows may go swift and far.*
> *Let your bending in the Archer's hand be for gladness;*
> *For even as He loves the arrow that flies, so He loves also the bow*
>   *that is the stable.*

Easier said than done no doubt. Yet here Kahlil Gibran offers such beauty, such inspiration to the parent as detached and loving custodian rather than being lost in ownership and vicarious living. My sister Donna is a wonderfully conscious mother and has often shared beautiful insights from Sarah Napthali's book *Buddhism For Mothers: a calm approach to caring for yourself and your children.* Donna swears this book is a truly sustaining support for contemporary mothers seeking to find more holistic ways of doing mothering.

Losing Ourselves in Work

Traditionally for men, and these days for women too, a similar phenomenon plays out within the domain of career. Out of duty, in the role identity of provider, men traditionally surrendered their sense of self to work.

Over time, the world of work became tenuous, fragile, uncertain which meant that they became such themselves. Jobs under threat, meant identity under threat. In the great depression and then the stock market crash of the 1980s, many men who lost their fortunes, lost themselves. They even committed suicide. In Australia in 2006-2007, the reported suicides of farmers is approximately one man every four days. For these men their entire sense of self is the land, the cattle, the crops, the generational identity of being a farmer. The drought has been so severe that as their crops don't yield, and their cattle die and their debts mount, the stress becomes so overwhelming that they choose the only way they can see out. They take their own lives.

Tragedy is one consequence of the Traditional Face. Its narrow definitions sometime gives very little choice. Looking through the eyes of this identity, there appears to be nothing else, no hope. The joy of the role is long gone and all that is left is the jail of a shrunken self from which there seems no escape.

And yet, the Traditional Face isn't always as traumatic, it can appear to work very well for some, and often for long periods of time. It is quite comforting to know your role and your place in the world, and if the prevailing system is kind and benevolent and you are well cared for, then you might be forgiven for living in denial of the limitations, for throwing your hands in the air and shouting: what's all the fuss about?

In Lithuania, a young woman brought her middle-aged

mother to The Four Faces weekend workshop. The mother really struggled to understand what we were talking about with the Traditional Face. She was exceptionally happy being a wife and a mother. She told us that her husband looked after her well, he cared for her, earned a good living, that she would be well provided for in the event of his death, that she liked cooking and cleaning and taking care of the family. She liked that he made all the big decisions. She was happy. Needless to say, she didn't come back on the second day.

And truly, the bliss of not having to think, of not having your whole sense of self thrown up in the air and exploded into myth, of not having to begin a committed journey of discovery, discovering who you really are after years and years of believing something other, the bliss of ignorance is definitely appealing. But it never lasts. Or if it does, it rarely lasts forever.

Nothing is static, and this kind of attitude doesn't help when the sands of change start to shift. I think an important question is, can this attitude in a mother help her children prepare for life in a world that is dynamic and ever-changing? And while existing in the feeling relative security is entirely understandable, is this denial the best way of playing this role?

Anything beyond 'I am' is vulnerable

Whenever we adopt a label as an identity, even the label of 'I am woman', we define ourselves within the norms, terms and context of cultures, religion, family, race. When we do this we lock ourselves into rules, roles and restrictions, we silence our conscience, we shrink our spirits. If however we decline to participate in what's expected of our externally defined selves, we run the risk of being outcast, excluded and denounced.

So why do we adopt external definitions, ultimately setting ourselves up as vulnerable?

Because we have forgotten who we are, we have become lost in form. But in order to feel secure which is perhaps the core underlying need, we must have some sense of self. And so we construct one…two…three…more. The irony is of course, in our attempt to feel secure, we make ourselves vulnerable, yet it is the best we can do.

I've learned over the years is to eliminate the labels of good and bad or right and wrong. Therefore The Traditional Face is not 'bad', it is not 'wrong', in fact, it is inevitable that we continue to live in its shadow as long as we are disconnected from our original selves. Perhaps the most effective way of working with the Traditional Face is by understanding its motivation. Fundamentally it attempts to provide security – physical, emotional, psychological and spiritual. This is not a bad motivation, it is natural as security is the core human need. Yet the modus operandi of the Traditional Face results only in conditional security, vulnerability with an accompanying range of costs to the spirit. It is not bad, it is just not effective.

Indeed, there is also nothing inherently bad or wrong with playing roles, or having possessions, taking care of your body, committing to relationships or making money. It is only when we lose our sense of self in these things which are external to our innate nature, that we become dependent and vulnerable, and as such under threat.

Then we live from fear… and that's not living. That's just surviving. And we're worthy of more than that.

It doesn't matter what labels you identify with, whether you are wealthy or a successful career woman or a struggling artist or a spiritual aspirant or a stay at home mum either supported or on welfare or an average woman experiencing both good times and bad or a super-mum. There is not a better or worse label to be attached to, they will all end in sorrow.

In twenty years of exploring this inner work, I've seen that all women experience frailty at some point or in some aspect of their lives. And some live with a baseline anxiety of being certain they will be 'seen', recognised as 'fake'. This was certainly my experience for some time and if this rings true for you too, maybe it is good to know you are not alone. Today there is a even name for it – The Impostor Syndrome.

It seems most executives suffer from it. In actual fact, we're all faking it to some extent. Yet as we reclaim our authenticity, our authentic power, we discover that we don't need to fake it, that we are amazing in our uniqueness, that our creative capacities are enormous. With each step that we take out of the Traditional Face, we get closer to realising the truth of who we were born to be. There is no need to copy or clone.

In all our simplicity and all our complexity we are competent and capable and remarkable. The Traditional Face is an illusion, promising a mere shadow of the vast treasure that we already are but have forgotten. It is just a matter of continually turning within and reconnecting with our authentic power and recovering our Eternal beauty.

Internally Defined

The Beginning

Eternal Face
'I am'

Traditional Face
'I am who you say
I am'
Conform to get...
Approval; Security; Belonging;
Acceptance; Love; Peace

Externally Defined

Thought Starters
The Traditional Face

What I get from adopting this Face.
- a sense of security
- feelings of belonging
- being accepted
- being loved
- I am part of a community, I am accepted, therefore I am safe, I am okay.

How this Face shapes my self-esteem.
- my self esteem is based on how well I adhere to the laws and to what degree I am accepted
- often my sense of self-esteem comes from feeling better than those who are 'outsiders'

What I sacrifice by wearing this Face.
- freedom
- truth
- pure creativity (quantum leaps as distinct from incremental variations on the past)
- inner knowing
- conscience
- individuality, uniqueness
- unfolding my destiny

What it costs me.
Unfettered Self Expression.

What sanskars (habits of personality) does it develop?
- defensiveness
- superiority/inferiority complex
- superstitious nature – fearful of what exists 'outside' the

boundaries
- judgementalism
- narrow/closed minded
- exclusivity
- rigidity
- potential fanaticism

How does the Traditional Face support and limit me?
It gives me an enormously strong foundation on which to build my life.
If I play by the rules, I am rewarded with great loyalty, encouragement and support.

An example is the Jewish community. It is purported that there are somewhere in the vicinity of ten million Jews worldwide and some of the most exquisite talents and minds in the arts, science and business have emerged from this culture.

It is a perfect example of the Traditional Face because it is a tradition that is deeply founded in law. The Ten Commandments were the beginning and the rules built from there.

There is a fantastic sense of belonging if you are Jewish... you can never 'not be Jewish' no matter what.

That gives a child a great head start in the world. However, if you are not Jewish, you never can be one.

There is an undeniably alluring quality about community, about the way each one looks after the other. A strong and stable foundation of love (conditional though it is), of knowing who you are and that you will be okay no matter what, is an extraordinary gift with which to begin one's life.

In India, this also holds true, especially for males. Boys begin life with the experience of being totally and wholly adored. They know without question that they are 'okay'. In the extended family, if your mother is not happy with you, or your father ignores you and favours another child, there's always an aunty or an uncle ready to give love and attention… and very often they live in the same house. This a tremendous baseline from which to start.

On the other hand, this same culture that makes the entry point to life so solid for boys, most often denies the same for the girl child. In other circumstances, it is genital mutilation, condoned incest, child slavery, imprisonment in hard labour by the church for having had pre-marital sex, murder by the father or brother for shaming the family, or merely that girls clean up in the house after their brothers. There are stories from all cultures, all religions, all traditions that show how this Face truly limits the natural expression and freedom of the soul's journey.

What feelings does it generate?
- fear
- comfort
- safety
- warmth
- being trapped
- loss and grief

What are its strengths?
- community
- support
- stability
- imperviousness
- confidence

What are its weaknesses?
- exclusivity
- groupthink
- bigotry
- narrow-mindedness
- control

What are its main drivers?
- security
- belonging
- acceptance
- love
- certainty

What are the main challenges?
- change
- accepting differences
- looking forward
- learning from 'outside' the tradition
- to be generous with outsiders without being conde-scending

How do I deal with change when wearing this Face?
- deny
- resist
- actively sabotage

What is the leadership capacity of the individual wearing the Traditional Face?
In our current climate, this Face is not a good leader. It will tell you why we don't need to change. It will look to the past for answers and will be unwilling to seek wisdom from other traditions, other sources. It will be fearful of the unknown and of course today, the future is completely uncertain. It doesn't live well with chaos, and needs to feel in control. Neither is the Traditional Face good with ambiguity or paradox. Because it has a tendency to 'stop rigorous thinking', it can find it extremely difficult to hold both ends of a spectrum, or opposites, and move toward integration.

How does this Face relate to power?
It has a hierarchical relationship to power. When wearing this Face there is always someone higher or lower on the power ladder. Position is power and with this face, we compete with each other, bow down to someone else or expect them to bow to us. Either way, it is clearly a misunderstanding of power. The power is in the system and the roles, not in the individual for their own worth.

What is its orientation to Time?
This is the Face that is inextricably linked to the past. It designs the present and the future based on what has gone before.

What is its relationship to emotion?
Because its foundation is the past, emotion is the domain of this Face. Emotions are the realm of remembering and comparing. Loss of what was, what has always been, can be devastating to this Face, therefore *fear of loss* is profoundly embedded within this face.

Because its identity is so much part of the collective, when something in the broader community changes, dies or is lost, then the individual naturally feels that pain.

However in this paradigm, certain emotions are acceptable for certain roles. Women can cry but they shouldn't be aggressive. Men can be angry but they shouldn't show sadness or vulnerability.

What is the prime addiction?
Pride. Appearances to 'outsiders' are everything. It won't allow anyone to know its secrets. What's wrong within the family, the religion, the organization, the clan... stays there. We don't talk about our problems outside. We are to be seen as perfect by all who would wish to glance our way.

How does this Face relate to God?

As protector, punisher, parent. If we follow all the rules and be good girls then we should be looked after. If we break the rules, then we are likely to incur the wrath of a God who as an extension of this face, is vindictive and punishing. God is often used as a tool in human power games. If we need to get people lower on the rung than us to obey, we can often put the 'fear of God' into them.

Because this world is limited, because it is strongly based on an identity that is to do with the physical world, with our bodies and with other human beings, then God too is a reflection of that. If God is powerful, then God is an authority, top of the hierarchy.

In religious environments (almost pure Traditional Face these days), we see human beings acting as 'God's representatives'. This elevates their power status and they are able to perform all range of matters in the name of God.

This Face also is the purveyor of wars 'in the name of God'. It protects its clan and if it is religiously formed then God will be the guide and protector. God will have the ultimate 'sign-off' on going to war. Of course it won't be God, but a human being interpreting through their own ego needs, using God's name to prove 'wrong to be right'.

Unfortunately it is this Face that gives God a bad name. It puts limits around the Unlimited. But it does not do it consciously or maliciously. God's identity and capacity is always contained within our own thinking, experiencing, living, loving, hoping and dreaming. Our limits have been formed by a combination of our own and others' life journeying – full of permutations and distortions over time when stories and rules have been edited for personal use or benefit.

There is no other choice but to see that if we are limited then our understanding and experience of God will be limited to only that which is imaginable or able to be experienced. And of course God will be way, way above, beyond our lowly selves. We will always be less, mere mortals, sinful and corrupt.

It is possible to believe that God will forgive me and will save me and if I follow the rules as best I can, then when I can't I might be excused.

With the Traditional Face it will be difficult to maintain a relationship of personal, intimate beauty with God, and yet, that is actually the very nature of our relationship with the Divine.

The Modern Face

The one who feels the pain and constriction of the Traditional Face, may then adopt the Modern Face to fight the boundaries, to run from them, seeking freedom.

Believing the limits to be outside, not recognising the resident resistor within, this face uses great energy to flee... but cannot. And while the Modern Face is etched from courage and commitment, it is unable to break free and create a new way because it is the face of reaction, its core energy discontentment born of the seed of tradition.

And from the seed grows the fruit. And from the fruit comes the seed...no escape.

Yet it is the first step.

Internally Defined

The Beginning

Eternal Face
'I am'

Modern Face
'I'm not who you say
I am'

Traditional Face
'I am who you say
I am'
Conform to get...
Approval; Security; Belonging;
Acceptance; Love; Peace

Externally Defined

THE MODERN FACE

"I'M NOT WHO YOU SAY I AM"

The circle of protection became a prison.
The modern face rebels, wants to break free from all the abuses of
power and rigidity expected in relationship to the role of a woman.
Thinker, freedom fighter, activist, sorcerer...
There have been many times where the world of inner feelings and
desires, the world of relationships is like a jungle incomprehensible and
contradictory...
Who am I? What do I want? Why am I unsatisfied? ...
Anger o Anger, where do you come from?
Valeriane Bernard

When you realise that you have lost yourself in the Traditions of
others, when you feel that who you are has been intrinsically
erased, when you no longer know what 'I' feel, what 'I' believe,
when you sense you have no power or freedom to be you, when
you awaken to the fact that you have simply adopted your
parents and peers thoughts, beliefs and opinions... anger erupts
and can be experienced as minor or intense... from annoyance
through to rage.

Usually we become angry with those who have shaped us...
family, religion, culture, spouse, institution. We no longer want
to be 'who you say I am' and we start to find our own voice... and
that voice is mad! ... "I am not who you say I am!" becomes the
cry, sometimes a whimper but still it can be heard if you are
listening. We rebel and we do that which is distinct or different
that which made us. We fight not to be what we were.

Unfortunately, that which we hunger for – truth and self-
expression – is not to be found in resistance, in what is effectively,
an anti-identity. The Modern Face is a struggle for power in a
powerless system of relationships. Much of our teenage years are

spent in this Face.

In it is seemingly more benign form, the Modern Face is the passive aggressive position of withdrawal. It rebels by non-participation, withholding discretionary energy, that is, the extra energy of joy, enthusiasm, love that one can bring to a role, a job, a task, a relationship.

I worked with a bank many years ago and in one session I asked the group to think about what they were passionate about. One woman shared with me and as she did, it is as if she came to life telling me about the beauty and accuracy of her needlepoint. I asked her how might she bring the essence of what she loved to create to work...not the needlepoint but the beauty and accuracy. Her face distorted into a mask of disdain and horror, blurting out "No way – they're not getting that!"

This was her passive aggressive stance, thinking that she was not giving them her power, when really she was robbing herself of that which gave her energy. The connection with her own essence. But in withholding, she was rebelling, reacting from her feeling of powerlessness to the domination of the big banking system. She was seeking to gain the power, the authority, the 'something' she had lost.

In its more obvious form, when someone wears the Modern Face they don the face of tremendous courage, of extraordinary stamina and of commitment to resurrecting a sense of the truth. This is the Face of the revolutionary, the rebel, the social reformer, the child who throws a tantrum refusing to be constrained any longer by someone else's rules.

It is the face of the freedom fighter, the egalitarian, the one who pursues justice and equal rights in reaction to the inconsistencies and injustices of the present – a legacy of the past traditions.

This face interrogates where it finds narrow mindedness. It confronts hierarchies and initiates coups. It is the reactive face, the one that moves forward on the basis of not accepting the status quo.

But beware, *I am not who you say I am* appears to move us

forward, and it can, but only as a first step in the process. If we stay caught in this rebellion, we are as lost as we felt we were in the Traditional face. If we don't wake up to this as an 'anti-identity' unfortunately it takes us no closer at all to the *I am* of the Eternal Face.

Without knowing the way forward, and in an attempt to reinvent ourselves, we reconstruct our lives. We create new rules, new ways, new systems. Very often they are as rigid in their intention as were the old rules. Lots of shoulds, shouldn'ts, musts and must nots.... Even if it is 'there should not be any rules' or 'everyone must be included'.

This is the face that gives birth to democracy over dictatorship, socialism over capitalism, feminism over patriarchy, adolescence rebelliousness, religious splits, any kind of political coup in an attempt for freedom.

By the very nature of the Traditional Face, the Modern Face must be cast out because when wearing it, we challenge the rules of the clan and the rules of the clan are inexorable, sacrosanct – they shape the individuals' identities. If we question the rules, we question the very existence of our 'family'. In effect, we call them liars, cheats and frauds.

On a personal level, the Modern Face robs me from my right to peace. I sacrifice love in hope of truth. I must close my heart to all that I had loved, that I feel betrayed by, if I am to have the courage to stand against it. And the freedom I think I am gaining, the truth I think I will discover are lost to blinding, driving emotion. I am not free at all, rather I am trapped by the rhythm of repulsion, and the truth is veiled once more because I have forbidden myself to embrace all of life. I have become as selective and narrow as that which I sought to leave behind. When wearing this face I compare what I am doing with the old – even at a subconscious level – telling myself and others that the new, what I – or we – have created, is much better.

What I can't see whilst wearing the *Modern Face* is that

although the externals may have changed, the invisible world that really drives everything is still the same. It is still a struggle for limited power, an attempt to feel secure and in control through a set of external constructs.

The *Modern Face* is simply the mirror image of the *Traditional Face* it opposes and despises so much.

In time, although we may not recognise this clearly, we certainly will feel dissatisfied...perhaps even as trapped, as contained, as we did in the Traditional Face, but we may not understand the cause. It is possible that we will ignore, even suppress the feelings that threaten to rob us of hope. But the old hunger for finding ourselves, for reconnecting with our truth, power and freedom that made us risk so much, will not go away.

If we're not awake to this story, we might push away again, blame again, use all our courage and energy again to start something new... again. Looking, searching, hungry. Becoming exhausted. Again. Going backwards instead of towards the dream.

And with so very much hope and good intention. Just with the wrong method. That's all.

The Good News

So if we continue to react against the system, the people and the control, then it is a great clue that we've not yet found our way home to ourselves. We are on the way, en route, we are undertaking the journey but we need a new method. And to do that, we need to let go of the fight. But the letting go is the tricky part. Sometimes we don't even realise how much we are 'holding on', how much we are resisting. It has become a way of life.

But there are ways, and you've already read about and practiced some from the Eternal Face chapter. Sometimes just reading this, recognising it, becoming aware is enough to begin the letting go. As my colleague Rob Mallick wrote to me: *The notion of the Modern face has "rocked my world". Just becoming aware of this archetype is, as you know, transformational."*

When we come to Shakti, there are a range of stories, tools and methods that give relief to the Modern Face while making sure to carry forward the greatness of this face.

A Different Way to Look at It

It is not possible as Einstein said, to solve existing world problems with the same level of thinking that created them. We need new thinking, which needs a new identity.

If the Eternal Face is the Original Form.

The Traditional Face is the face that Conforms.

Then the Modern Face is the face that Reforms… it is not a new form, simply a reforming of the conformist system.

The new thinking, the new identity needs to be one that transcends our existing systems, one that provides us with detachment, a bird's eye view, a whole system perspective giving us the power to return to our pure selves, the Original Form. And this face will understand that to move forward, to create a world for myself and others that is worth living in, I will need to transform my thinking, my consciousness first. I need to reorient my awareness, my sense of self to a state that is stable, a state that is anchored in a lasting truth, not a malleable set of external constructs.

I will need to cultivate my mind and my heart and align them to an authentic state of being, a resonance of my own truth. When my thoughts, my feelings and actions are an expression of my eternal truth, then transformation unfolds.

And finally, it is useful to know how to access power from an unlimited source of pure energy, rather than being continually caught in the power struggles of day to day human existence. Being independent and sharing the beauty, the creativity and inspiration with others by being, is a way to influence a new world from a pure seed. Then surely, the fruit of that seed will be pure also?

Internally Defined

The Beginning

Eternal Face
'I am'

Modern Face
'I'm not who you say
I am'
Push back to get...
Freedom; Independence;
Creativity; Truth; Power;
Self-Expression

insecure

Traditional Face
'I am who you say
I am'
Conform to get...
Approval; Security; Belonging;
Acceptance; Love; Peace

Externally Defined

Thought Starters
The Modern Face

What I get from adopting this Face
   Bursts of Energy
   A renewed sense of self.
   Confidence
   The illusion of empowerment
   A feeling of freedom
   Excitement
   A new identity (not Traditional identities)

How this Face shapes my self-esteem.
I begin to identify with the righteousness of the cause for which I take a position and as such I feel righteous. I start to measure myself very much in comparison to others but always as superior.

What I sacrifice by wearing this Face.
   I sacrifice security, home, belonging, acceptance, support, stability, love.
   Although within the *Traditional Face* these are conditional, if I am to be true to my cause, I must renounce them. I will seek to create all of these again in the new domain that I create in opposition to the *Traditional Face,* and they too will be conditional. The Modern Face will in time, revert and become Traditional.

What it costs me (all conditional)
   Peace of mind
   Openness of heart
   Stability
   Belonging
   Security

What sanskars (habits of personality) does it develop?
  Restlessness
  Critical intellect – always noticing what's wrong

How does the Modern Face support and limit me?
It supports me in giving me a sense of independence. It makes me feel that I am not merely living at the behest of someone else's terms and conditions.

It limits me in draining maximum amounts of my energy into a false sense of self and security.

What feelings does it generate?
  Anger
  Resentment
  Hatred
  Righteousness
  Freedom
  Independence

What are its strengths?
  Courage
  Determination
  Innovation
  Vision

What are its weaknesses?
  Arrogance
  Projection (external focus, rarely looking at the self)
  Limited (often rejects even the good in what it opposes)

What are its main drivers?
  Need for a sense of power
  Need for freedom
  Need for truth

Need for unfettered self-expression

What are the main challenges?
Hopelessness
Depression
Tiredness
...because everything I try to do, all the changes I try to make,
never really work.
Being outcast – separation/isolation
Loneliness
Insecurity

How do I deal with change when wearing this Face?
Usually I would be the one or one of the ones driving the change
and as such I would feel in control and somewhat powerful.
However, if someone else tries to impose change on me when I'm
wearing this face, I am likely to resist, challenging their
capability. If I can become part of the change, helping to drive it,
I will cooperate. If not, I may even sabotage the change.

*What is the leadership capacity of the individual wearing the
Modern Face?*
For a time, it appears that this face has leadership potential. It can
often rally resources and people for it is change cause. It knows
how to speak to the unsatisfied souls and inspire people to a new
way.

However, when the woman wearing this face finally realises
that nothing has really transformed, only simply changed appearances – for example, communism from capitalism – simply a
different group have the money and the power.

When the realization occurs that all the effort that has been
made hasn't really liberated anyone, there can be a sense of
hopelessness, despondency and tiredness. At this point 'giving
up' is a natural option, in which case the leadership potential is

spent. If on the other hand the woman wearing this face continues to 'project', to blame the external systems for her pain and disappointment, she will react again against the system and lurch again into a new way forward, with a new fad. Too many times doing this, her followers will stop trusting her leadership capacity.

How does this Face relate to power?

This face hungers for power. The woman wearing this face either has no position in the hierarchy of tradition, or has managed to play the game, climb the hierarchical ladder, only to find the power she thought she would find there, is not there. She gets angry and disillusioned and rather than 'own' how it is, she blames the system for her feeling of powerlessness and reacts... donning the Modern Face.

What is its orientation to Time?

The Modern Face is very future-focused, thus giving it its restless nature. If I am wearing this face I will find it very difficult to enjoy today, to relax, to be at peace... always thinking things should be different, planning for the next step. I will have denied the past, often suppressed it, yet it will be that past that will subconsciously drive my thoughts and my actions.

Everything I *don't want* will be held in the past. Everything I *do want* will be measured by what I *don't want*. I think I am escaping my past, but in fact, I am shaping my future from all that I detest. Anti-apartheid in South Africa was at its essence a part of the system of Apartheid and as such, they couldn't destroy Apartheid without destroying themselves... which they naturally couldn't do. It wasn't until they understood this and moved to define The Third Thing – which became known as Nationhood – that the country's systems began to transform. It was a creative process rather than a reactive one.

What is its relationship to emotion?
This face is driven by emotion, but mostly recognises the head. If I am wearing this face, I will plan and strategise. Emotions such as anger and excitement will be present, but I will have lost connection with the gentle emotions or feelings, often seeing these as weak.

What is the prime addiction?
Self-righteousness. This face thinks it knows how to fix what it perceives to be wrong and the person who wears it believes that she is the one to do it.

How does this Face relate to God?
There are perhaps two main ways in which this face perceives God. Having viewed what might be interpreted as the mindless manner in which others have related with God through the Traditional Face – 'blind faith' – this face will often denounce God as a mere 'need' of those who are too weak to stand on their own feet.

The Modern Face can misinterpret authenticity and independence, living from an arrogant self-reliance and therefore shun God.

On the other hand, in religious environments, it may Decide that it is God's will that I be instrument the one to shine divine light on the new contemporary way forward.

The Face of the Shakti

It is the Face of the Shakti that holds the secret key which unlocks the door to authenticity, beauty and power - freedom. It is this face which sees the limitations of tradition, but it has the capacity to take responsibility and reclaim power. It does not react nor does it blame.

It is able to detach and see that we are all caught in the web of reaction and that one can keep pointing the finger of fault and the pointing has no end.

The Shakti comes to 'see' herself and the systems in which she plays with wisdom and without judgment.

Her purpose-filled action sends silent ripples of pure energy to resurrect her essence and transform the old and ailing systems.

Transformation begins.

Internally Defined

Shakti -
Empowered Face
'I access the Power to
be who I am'

The Beginning

Eternal Face
'I am'

Modern Face
'I'm not who you say
I am'
Push back to get...
Freedom; Independence;
Creativity; Truth; Power;
Self-Expression

insecure

Traditional Face
'I am who you say
I am'
Conform to get...
Approval; Security; Belonging;
Acceptance; Love; Peace

Externally Defined

SHAKTI – THE EMPOWERED FACE

"I HAVE THE POWER TO BE WHO I AM"

Freedom from fear and sorrow, freedom from anger and injustice comes
from being in the right space inside....
Connected to inner eternal powers and reencountering Divinity....
It is accessible, it is a reality I can gently remind myself of my own
capacity to be free and powerful, in a space where love and beauty
don't ware a human face. I can awaken in me the Shakti face.
Valeriane Bernard

Shakti is derived from the oldest language on earth, Sanskrit. It has been adopted by one of the oldest cultures on earth, India. Shakti has three different, yet interconnected meanings.

- Power
- God's creative energy
- Divine feminine – the Goddess archetypes of the Hindu pantheon are called Shaktis

The Time for Shakti

There are many stories of Shaktis, of the divine feminine remembered as having restored harmony to the world through their sacred powers. These stories don't exist only in the Eastern traditions. These stories can be found in myths from cultures right across the world.

Experts in mythology such as Mircea Eliade, tell us that mythology is the telling of events that happened in primordial time...that is with human beings in the beginning of our world. If this is so, and if we work within the context of time being circular, cyclic, then it is possible that what we are remembering in our mythology is this time of great transformation that we are in right now. That we are recalling not the benevolent acts of ethereal beings, rather we are re-emerging the time when women moved beyond the limitations of our narrow-minded systems and worked together at a higher order of thinking and being to bring about transformation.

The question is how? How did we do it? How can we do it again...now?

A Change of Identity

The ability to transcend the existing form, the current systems that disempower us, transforming them to a better way, a more harmonious, just world, first requires each of us to transcend our old thinking. According to physics:

It is not possible to solve any problem from the level of consciousness or thinking that created it. And each one's thinking is born solely and absolutely from her identity.

We've seen already that identity is a complex matter, born of lifetimes of conforming and rebelling, and perhaps most of all, this lifetime of identifying as a woman.

The challenge presented by identifying with our gender is that we are both consciously and subconsciously shaped and driven by millennia of what it means to be 'woman'... the good, the great, the limited and the destructive.

If we are to find ways to change our thinking, to transform our actions, to feel powerful enough to create the life we want for ourselves, our families and our world, then it is essential to find a new identity that is free from the conditioning of the past thousands of years.

If we are to return to our Eternal selves, that which we continually yearn for, constantly try to connect with, then perhaps that is where we must start ... 'be that which I seek'.

The Journey from Gross to Subtle

We are used to focusing on what our senses perceive, to identifying with what we can see and feel and hear, with what exists in the physical world. We look at the effect and forget to seek out the cause. We look at such social problems as hunger, poverty and abuse and we look to fix those problems by providing aid or attack those who seem to be creating the problems.

Today there is the move to educate communities and people in need in different areas such as agriculture and finance and resource management which is better than keeping nations dependent, but it is still dealing with the problem and not the cause. Rarely do we trace the cause back to the subtle world of identity and thought.

If at a soul level we're feeling insecure, threatened or unsafe, we will hoard money, food and other resources to provide for a possible future of scarcity. If we feel insecure, we will form egoistic identities to feel good about ourselves. These identities will require a lot of maintenance, with some needing a range of material resourcing to reinforce their longevity – the Georgian mansion, imported car, designer labels, more shoes than a person needs in one lifetime, cosmetics, plastic surgery...and so on.

We can make a donation to World Vision and sponsor a child in Africa, with forty dollars a month, providing food and schooling and receiving a photo and letters so that we feel we are doing something at least. But essentially, our world is one of a race who is insecure, self-protective, self-interested, first and foremost, and who tries to feel secure by using the means of the material world.

In longing to return to the security of the Eternal self – offering us love, power, peace, purity, joy, truth – we've forgotten where to look. We have forgotten that the subtle, the invisible is where it all begins – the world of inner thoughts and feelings.

Everything is created first in the subtle world of thought and imagining. That who I am exists without anyone else's interpretation, defamation or exultation. I am because I am. And I know who I am. (Internal referral).

In Conformist mode (The Traditional Face), we are identifying as part of a broader group and our thinking and behaviour will be a correlate of that identification. We will think and act according to the rules of the group, under the illusion that by so doing, we will remain safe.

In this model, we become the dutiful woman – the subservient wife and mother or we manipulate power or seek it wherever we can find it, usually through position within the family, social or professional structure. Once position is attained, the young women who are 'below' us can pose a threat to the limited power we perceive in the system and so they are kept powerless as we were. In this mode, I identify outside of myself and I keep the system alive.

(External referral).

In Reformist mode (Modern Face), we dis-identify with the group. Identity is then an anti-identity, which by definition and form is still part of the same system. As such, thinking and behaviour will manifest as a polarity to its traditions... they will be the yin to its yang... the opposite, the tension of the 'other' that also keeps the system alive.

Having sought to be free, I can never be free because I carry the system I abhor within my heart and my mind. All actions are either consciously or subconsciously driven by attachment (my disdain) to the system. My sense of self is in relation to the changes I am making. (External referral)

A New Identity
In Transformist mode (Shakti), I access the power to redefine myself not based on anything external, rather on the authentic call from within. I begin the journey of recognising that I can reclaim the powers and virtues of the Eternal self, and can then impact the world outside. In fighting the existing system I give it my power.

By turning within, I am able to regenerate my energy, hear what I know to be real, understand right action, tap creativity, become fearless, know my destiny.

The world around me becomes a mirror to check my progress, to see myself. As I change my form, my thinking, my inner capacities, my world will shift accordingly.

Where there is pure and powerful *intention* followed by *attention*, I will see this reflected in my physical environment – personal hygiene, home and work space, personal and professional relationships, physical health and wellbeing, happiness, prosperity. If my outer world is stuck, it is telling me that my inner world is stuck.

Shakti is the face that transforms the world through deep attention to the inner world. As the woman who wears this face, I know that focusing on external causes and fights is to avoid looking at my own addictions, my own needs, my own unhealed self. To put all attention on the injustices of the world, is to feed them with what little power I have left.

As Shakti I experiment with the subtle, the spiritual, I test the principles and laws of life and see that the invisible world of thoughts and feelings is directly responsible for the outcomes I see in my outer world. I learn to trust my intuition once it is honed with spiritual power.

In the face of opposition I learn not to fight, rather to put power behind my intuitive knowing. I understand that the opposition comes to steal my power because it feels threatened. The fight is started to distract me from my vision, my focus and as such, I am not deluded, rather I stay firm in my new identity and access my inner powers and qualities keeping fixed on my course. (Internal referral – External check).

Shakti is Power

The simple exercise of shifting identity from woman to Shakti gives the experience of becoming free and powerful. The challenge is to let go of thousands of years of conditioning that says that women are...

- less
- stupid
- impure
- irrational
- gateway to hell
- objects of lust
- possessions or servants to men.

The challenge is to stop believing in who the existing world tells me I am and to withdraw into remembering who I really am.

The very act of withdrawing my focus from the external to the internal begins the journey of transcendence.

* I am no longer a woman (a physical identity), I am Shakti – the divine feminine... an instrument for God's energy, God's transformative work in the world.

* I am no longer limited in my role as a mother, I become a World Mother sharing my love, tolerance and protective powers with all the human world family.

Understanding the System

The existing world system (generally speaking) is patriarchal, the system of male domination, where those born as men are born with the right to rule. This system has been empowered generation after generation, in cultures the world over. This system of domination, of power over another, is then adopted by everyone within the system. Women dominate other women to regain the power that has been taken by (and given away to) the men within the system.

In 2005 before I left Australia, I heard Mary Robinson speak. She was wonderfully inspiring, telling many great stories about her life during and beyond being the time when she was the first woman president of Ireland. Her term lasted seven years. She was followed by another woman, who was halfway through her second term in 2005, when I was told this story.

Mary Robinson told us she knew a woman who had an eleven year old son. This son had said to her one day, "Mum, can a boy ever be president?" We usually know the story from the other side: can a girl ever be president?

This story shows me that our human consciousness system has bred into it the system of dominance based on difference, born out of insecurity.

The system of dominance is a system of powerlessness, of working with limited amounts of energy. It is structured on the subconscious basis that there is only a certain amount of energy available to us and it is a system of taking power from others because we don't know how else to replenish ourselves.

When we act from a body identity of male or female, we are bound by the system of the physical, the laws that apply to the physical universe.

However if we transcend this system of limited consciousness, embodying our original identity of subtle energy, virtues, powers, spirit... then we have access to energy outside and beyond the limitations of this system.

As we change our identity, becoming more secure in our sense of self, we move the limits and remove the border delineations, seeing ourselves and others as whole beings of possibility and power.

If we are secure in ourselves and powerful, we don't feel threatened, we don't become defensive, there is peace. Indeed we can become conduits to imbue the limited human system with divine energy, Shakti, enabling ourselves and others to return to the being of the Eternal Face.

The Way of Being Shakti
The Way is both simple and complex... and it is a process. The simplicity is in knowing that it is merely a shift in identity. The complexity is in holding that shift constantly over a long period of time.

Simple:

I am soul, spirit, light, energy.

I am the power that generates my life.

I am the subtle, the cause, the intention, the creator.

I am love, peace, truth, beauty, divinity.

I am that which I seek.

I live within this perishable body of matter, the point source of consciousness energising the brain and body from the seat of the third eye.

Complex:

We continue to become embroiled in the limitations of Tradition or Modernity because we identify with the physical, buying into the system of domination, of power games and struggles between genders, hierarchies, cultures, religions, clans, groups and so on.

However when we recognise and understand this, then each one of us can continually make and reaffirm the conscious choice to access power from another source.

The Way of being Shakti involves three steps.

1. The art and discipline of remembering that I am that which I seek... I am soul... all that is subtle... beauty, love and power.
2. The active and full participative relationship with the divine, with God, the replenishing source of power.
3. Being receptive to 'guidance' and trusting that I am an instrument for transformational change, I take action in the world

So how does all this work in a practical way? Between saying 'yes' and doing it, there's bound to be a gap to some degree. So, how do we close the gap?

After recognizing, understanding and realising, comes learning. In learning theory there are four steps to integrating the learning.

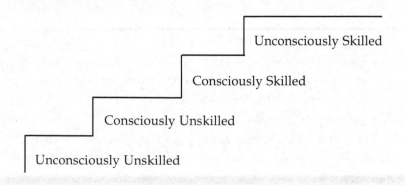

Unconsciously Unskilled is of course the time when we are asleep, without any awareness about how life works, that we have thoughts that create our lives, that we are subservient to external stimuli, and so on.

Then we wake up and become Consciously Unskilled, that is we become aware of some things, and aware that we are inept, unable, without skill, method or power. It is important to recognize that this step is a natural part of the learning process, it helps us to recognize that we want to learn, to change, to gather more ability to be in charge. So while becoming aware means that we sometimes feel 'oh my God...what a mess!' it is an essential step.

I remember thinking that my thoughts after I started to meditate were far more vicious, peaceless and destructive than previously, until I realised that before meditating I just had absolutely no awareness of my inner world at all.

So it is normal to be somewhat shocked at what you see when you become conscious. And it is good motivation to make the necessary steps to go to the next stage. It is also important to remember this isn't a one-off process. You will continue to wake up to new aspects of yourself the whole way along the journey.

Then comes the Consciously Skilled part. This is the step in which you start learning, practicing and experimenting. You try and check the results. You hear, see and feel and then whatever comes to you in the form of knowledge, you make your own. And then you integrate it into yourself. You see how it fits and if it does, you allow it to resonate with your very essence. Sometimes the knowledge comes before the timing is right. If something doesn't make sense, if it doesn't resonate, then just leave it aside. If it is right for you, it will be right in the right time. And if the time is right, you integrate and then... You become.

This is the final step. Unconsciously Skilled. You have become the learning. It has become you. You are one. The knowledge becomes your experience, which is your authority. You don't need a piece of paper or a title, your authority is unquestionable, because it is power is truth, authenticity.

So in the next few chapters, we will cover a variety of different tools, insights, practices and methods that will enable you to continually learn, become and be.

The Different Aspects of Shakti

In order to break down a little the role of Shakti, we will look at three different areas of Intelligence:

- Emotional – self and other awareness.
- Spiritual – who am I? what am I here for?
- Creative – the law of manifestation.

The Shakti's role of transformation means she works with the energy of '3'-

- three Faces – Eternal, Traditional, Modern
- three intelligences – Emotional, Spiritual, Creative
- three aspects of time – Present, Past, Future
- three energies of manifestation – Detach, Dream, Do
- three energies of transformation – Creation, Sustenance, Destruction
- She uses the third eye in order to see clearly.

Shakti becomes the Alchemist, turning the shadows into light and the alloy into gold.

Shakti is a very active role. A proactive role, nurtured and strengthened in silence... where knowledge becomes wisdom and wisdom becomes experience.

Thought Starters
The Face of Shakti

What I get from adopting on to this Face.
- Security
- Freedom
- Access to truth
- Love
- Peace
- Power
- Happiness
- The purity of my own being

How this Face shapes my self-esteem.
- It delivers me to my own source of self – to the core of truth and beauty.
- It is the face that returns me to self-esteem, to self-respect, self-confidence.

What I sacrifice by wearing this Face.
- Attachment to the way things have been.
- Limited attainment and achievement.
- Addiction or attachment to temporary support.
- Not taking responsibility for myself and my life.

What it costs me.
Initially it can cost me acceptance and peace as my loved ones will wonder what is happening, why I am changing and why I am causing disturbance in their lives. Sometimes this will mean that they project their dissatisfaction and insecurity onto me. If I'm not

aware that this could happen, I don't have any strategies for managing myself and supporting them through the changes.

However, being conscious, I can use the 8 Powers to maintain my stability and in my meditation and throughout the day I can send my loved ones positive stabilising energy.

In time they may even look to me for guidance if they can see my contentment, my success, they will feel my strength and my love and as long as I don't try to 'convert' them, it is likely they will want to feel it too.

What sanskars (habits of personality) does it develop?
- Pure independence and interdependence
- Non-judgement
- Cooperation
- Tolerance
- Love
- Mercy
- Assertiveness
- Clarity
- Discernment
- Decisiveness
- Creativity
- Responsiveness
- Intuition
- Determination
- Focus
- Trust
- Joyfulness
- Appreciation
- Stillness
- Wisdom
- Generosity
- Accuracy
- Respect

- Integrity
- Authenticity
- Purity
- Responsibility
- Humility

How does the Face of the Shakti support and limit me?
It supports me in returning to my Original Form, my Eternal self, the subtle qualities I seek in every action I perform, in every day of my life.

It limits me in that the ordinary and mundane no longer satisfy me, even if I persist with them.

How I spend my time changes as I feel the power of the Shakti calling me to my destiny.

Once awakened, it is very hard to go to sleep again and so if I slip into ordinariness and resist the call, I will have to suppress my inner voice, denying of my own truth. Eventually I will have to feel the consequences of not giving regard to my own knowing.

What feelings does it generate?
- Strength
- Compassion
- Faith
- Certainty
- Ease

What are its strengths?
- Unshakeable
- Steadfastness
- Vision
- Wisdom
- Acceptance
- Love
- Silence

What are its weaknesses?
There are none. In the journey back to myself I will certainly behave out of weakness but this is not to be attributed to the Shakti, rather I have forgotten again and slipped back to either Traditional or Modern.

What are its main drivers?
It is not driven or compelled.

When I wear this face I am inspired to my own truth, my own destiny, to return to the home of the self.

I am also inspired to contribute to humanity as part of my destiny, to find my purpose for being here at this time, with these choices.

What are the main challenges?
- Not reverting to old patterns as unconscious reactions to circumstances.
- To balance all powers and not become dependent on just a few.
- To balance time for the self, and time for others.
- Confusing old Modern Face thinking and behavior with Shakti (it requires great honesty with the self and a very subtle understanding which comes from reflection and stillness).
- Making time in the day to nurture silence within.
- To take my nourishment from the Source and not from people, things, activities, roles, achievements, consumables.

How do I deal with change when wearing this Face?
I embrace change, I allow it to flow into my life knowing it to be a sign that I am on track.

What is the leadership capacity of the individual wearing the Face of the Shakti?
This is the face of the Transformational Leader, the kind of leader needed in today's world.

- To be bold enough to trust the invisible world of virtues, powers and inner knowing.
- To stand on the path without a map, with only an internal compass, intuition and signals from the universe to guide me.
- To stand for principles and liberation when others are acting from fear.
- To know absolutely that love is *the* greatest transformational power there is...
- ...That humility is a strength and arrogance is weakness...
- ...That a divine intellect is a completely practical intellect...
- ...That a still mind is pure creative resource...
- ...This is the kind of leadership needed to bring about a world that is sustainable. It is a leadership that can, will and does happen at all levels of society.

How does this Face relate to power?
It is power and as such has no need to try and take power from others. Wearing this face I donate power because I am in connection with the Supreme Source of power. In giving I do not lose power, I rejuvenate and regenerate.

What is its orientation to Time?

- This is the Face that sits across the three aspects of time...
- In wearing this face I am able to live fully in the present and enjoy the benefits of 'being'.
- I am aware of where I have come from and to where I am going.
- I learn from the past so that the present can be the best it can be, understanding that my actions today will have conse-

quences tomorrow.

- I work with the future, creating a pure vision for myself and my world, a vision that supports me by pulling me forward and away from the magnetic pull of past patterns.
- It inspires my thinking, my choices and my actions today.

Eventually when I have practiced wearing this face enough, I will have become my Eternal self once again. At that time, I will live naturally, unconsciously in 'now'.

My thoughts and actions will merge as oneness. I will be the embodiment of responsiveness, of right action...manifestation of thought into action will be a clean and clear and natural process.

Along the journey I will experience moments, days, weeks in this state, until I am hijacked by survival Faces. Then the game is to return easily to the higher state without lament or sorrow for the temporary loss.

What is its relationship to emotion?
If we define emotion as energetic reactions to external stimulus to which I am attached, this face is beyond emotion because it is beyond reaction and attachment. Pure feelings are the domain of Shakti.

What is the prime addiction?
The one who wears it can become addicted to transformation. The purpose of transformation is to eventually become, not to eternally transform. The addiction can be continual motion, analysis, change, process, never stopping to just be and enjoy the being.

How does this Face relate to God?
The relationship with God when wearing this face is one of partnership. I understand that God is powerful and wondrous and magnificent because God has never forgotten.

The more time I spend connecting with God, with this source

of pure energy and beauty, the more I realize that this is my own intrinsic nature. My relationship with God is one of being taught, guided, loved into becoming equal. I also realise that there is no dependency, no debt, no sorrow in this connection.

As the Source, I'm able to experience all relationships with this One... the unique energy of a mother, a teacher, a lover, a friend, a playmate, a father, a comforter of my heart.

All my soul needs can be satisfied in this connection which means I can clean my energy, purify my being, allowing me to be in relationship with others in a completely non-dependent, non-needy, non-taking manner.

In Shakti, my relationship with God is intelligent and sensitive. I know that God is a constantly benevolent being of light. Only when I slip into lower energy or frequency thoughts and actions do I disconnect myself from that Source. Otherwise, the flow of pure energy, of continual blessings, of powerful vision is constant and fully available for me. And this is the most exquisite reward for undertaking this journey.

SHAKTI MASTERS THE NEW INTELLIGENCES

I grew up in an era when intelligence was measured by IQ. As we've learned over the years, IQ (Cognitive Intelligence) is a way of measuring a very small portion of the neurological capacity. It is the measurement primarily of the ability to effectively use the logical, linear, verbal, mathematical left brain. Research indicates the delineation of learning and knowing capacities is more complex than simply slicing the brain down the middle and referring to left and right hemispheres, however for ease, this is usually the way in which it is referred.

Left Hemisphere
- Logic
- Needs Structure
- Linear Processing
- Sequential
- Mathematics
- Words
- Concrete

Right Hemisphere
- Creativity
- Accommodates Chaos
- Intuition
- Holistic Processing
- Random
- Symbolic
- Pattern recognition
- Visionary

It is apparent even from this sketchy overview, that IQ really deals with a very narrow perspective on intelligence.

When I was in the south of Brazil in Canela, there was a woman at a Four Faces workshop who shared that one of the reasons she was at the workshop was that she wanted to increase her memory through meditation. When I questioned her a little more, she said that she had always felt stupid, that she wasn't as intelligent as others and had heard that meditation can improve your brain's ability, specifically with memory and with numbers. It turns out this woman is a talented artist, she's an inspired mother, a brilliant dressmaker, story teller, sports coach and has many other talents.

I told her that meditation can definitely improve memory and can help us to access more of our brain's capacity. And most importantly I hoped I helped her to understand that what she was hoping to develop was only one kind of intelligence, not *the* intelligence. That there are many different kinds of intelligence, it is just that most of our education systems worldwide educate the masculine, 'left' hemisphere, and then measure each person's aptitude in that area and call it intelligence. This is a very limited and limiting view of intelligence.

Howard Gardner codified nine intelligences, arguing that for a full, well rounded education that prepared us for a genius life, we needed to develop all nine. These are:

- Logical-mathematical
- Linguistic
- Musical
- Visual/Spatial
- Bodily-kinesthetic
- Interpersonal
- Intrapersonal
- Naturalist
- Existential

It does help to be intelligent in IQ because our external world is built on it, however times are changing.

Daniel Goleman launched a body of work entitled *Emotional Intelligence* in the late 1990s. Since then there has been Dana Zohar's expose on *Spiritual Intelligence*, there is *Adversity Intelligence*, *Creative Intelligence* and *Divine Intelligence*. Recently in Chile, there was an article about a book being written on *Maternal Intelligence*.

While we could be considered a little dull and unimaginative in repeating the intelligence 'code', it seems to me that there is a natural need in the human psyche at this time to acknowledge the value and validity of a number of different ways of being considered intelligent.

The New Intelligences Reunite the Masculine and Feminine Energies Within Everyone

The new intelligences highlight the value and validity of the 'softer', more invisible capabilities, especially in these times of enormous change. The qualities associated with the right hemisphere are typically codified as feminine energy, while the more logical, tangible, left brain capacities are referred to as masculine energy.

The process of rebalancing the two energies in our world and in ourselves is at the heart of the spiritual journey.

In Eastern mythology there is a symbol for the perfect balance of the masculine and feminine within each individual. In Indian culture it is seen in Vishnu... the four armed image which is said to be the energy of sustainability, and in the Chinese tradition there is the Tao of the Yin and Yang symbol. In Buddhism, we have the Buddha and Kuan Yin, the feminine form of the Buddha.

Carl Jung talked about the Anima and Animus within each of us. In the Roman and Greek mythologies, there are masculine and feminine archetypes – the Gods and Goddesses symbolising the balance of energies within human beings.

When we talk about Shakti, we can talk about Shiva-Shakti which is the combined form of Shiva and Shakti, of masculine divinity and feminine divinity.

The new intelligences are about returning to these archetypal balances, to embodying within ourselves the pure energies of both the feminine and the masculine energies. It is not possible for this balance to exist in our world unless it first exists within each of us. We will still play the roles of men and women, but from a wholeness, a fullness, that makes us secure and powerful, allowing us to let go of fear, enabling us to be more generous, more loving, more trusting, more compassionate and more creative.

In the next few pages, I will introduce Emotional, Spiritual and Creative Intelligences as they relate to the spiritual journey in the context of The Four Faces.

If you want to explore these intelligences further, then you will easily find vast volumes on EQ (Emotional Intelligence) and SQ (Spiritual Intelligence) and some on CQ (Creative Intelligence).

Emotional Intelligence

Emotional Intelligence has been classified in a range of different ways, the most popular coming from Daniel Goleman's book *Emotional Intelligence*. Goleman's work is primarily based in the arena of business and leadership development and much of his research in association with the Hay Group, highlights that EQ is the difference that makes a leader in today's market. They show clearly that IQ might get you the job, but EQ gets you promoted.

Their research shows that significant strengths in:

- Analytical reasoning added 50% more incremental profit.
- Self management competencies added 78% more incremental profit.
- Social skills added 110% incremental profit.
- Social skills + self management added 390% incremental profit.

Even though in this book, we are not focusing at all on business, on career or on money, we are focused on the real and tangible results that The Four Faces journey and tools produce. The above statistics are examples of how working with inner capacities is becoming more valued and recognised, even in the last bastion of left brain dominance, the domain of business.

So for those who are not familiar with EQ, effectively there are four areas. I have adapted the following from Goleman et al.

Self awareness
- Knowing your own emotions
- Knowing your patterns – positive and destructive

Self management
- Maintaining a level of detachment from old patterns
- Managing your own emotions
- Being authentic in who you are today

- Motivating yourself

Social awareness
- Recognizing the feelings of others
- Making a contribution
- Having awareness of the systems in which you exist

Relationship management
- Understanding and managing relationship dynamics
- Identifying and articulating needs and expectations in relationship
- Supporting and inspiring others
- Managing transformation in relationship

Spiritual Intelligence

Effectively this entire book is dedicated to developing Spiritual Intelligence (SQ). SQ is about self awareness but awareness beyond the perfunctory management of daily life like EQ. SQ proposes that there is...

- a greater meaning
- a greater context
- and a greater purpose to each life in which we are all connected... to our own divinity, to each other's divinity and to the Source of Divinity.

SQ is about re-emerging and revitalizing
- the original qualities or virtues of the soul (see The Eternal Face)
- and developing the powers of the soul (see Shakti Face).

SQ asks the profound questions of life...
- Who am I?
- Why am I here?
- Who or what or is God?

Unlike EQ, which says I have to become better, SQ says I just need to be my authentic self and that is powerful. It works on the basis that inherent in each one of us is the blueprint of 'being', pure and perfect. It suggests that if we can learn the arts of introspection and stillness, invocation of pure innate qualities from within, silent and deep connection to the Supreme Source that reminds us we are created in that likeness... together with the energetic science of alchemical transformation, then we are able to return to the fullness of our own unique being.

From this state, we contribute well beyond daily tasks or even exemplary performance. In this state we carry the energy of 'heaven' within and just by being in that state, we start to invoke the same memories in others with whom we connect.

Creative Intelligence (CQ)

The natural state of the human is soul is one of unique creative expression. Only when we disconnect from our eternal security and we start to depend on others to feel secure, do we begin to compromise and lose this innate capacity. As we grow older within our education system, we tend to become less creative, and so we lose our abilities to innovate.

Sally used to teach. She told me that whenever she would ask a group of five year old children "Who can sing?" They would all shoot up their hands and shout "Me!!!" "Who can dance?" Again, a chorus of "Me!!!!!!"

In the workshops, lectures and seminars that I lead, when I ask the same questions, I'm lucky if one percent of the room respond in the positive. Mostly I hear groaning and 'Oh no!'

Creative Intelligence is not about being an acclaimed artist, rather it is about living life as an art. It is about expressing your uniqueness unabashedly, with the joy that comes from no external constraints. But today we are told to "be appropriate". The question that comes to my mind is "appropriate according to whose criteria?" As we grow older, we tend to become more conservative, more cautious, more fearful and more insecure. The frailty of body feeds back to us that we need to be careful, we might fall, get attacked, become ill, have a heart attack. And so before we die, we stop living. Out of insecurity and fear, we shrink our world and lose the art of living.

CQ reconnects us to this lost art. It is about divining our future in alignment to our most precious essence. It is about understanding the law of manifestation; the dimensions and the energies of transformation and then using the 8 Powers to clear the way, moving with the river of newness as it flows through our lives.

TOOLS FOR DEVELOPING FOR EMOTIONAL, SPIRITUAL AND CREATIVE INTELLIGENCE

Emotional, Spiritual and Creative Intelligence – EQ, SQ and CQ – all share similar tools. When you reach different levels in practice, the tools transform and become more like powers, weapons, magic. It is the same process for a chef, a tennis player, a writer. We all have the same components to play with, to use, to wield, however it is our skill, our experience, our practice, our energy that creates functionality, art or alchemy.

Breathing
In a busy day and life, we can tend to move through emotional barrages without resolving or releasing the energy. This 'energy in motion' gets stored as trapped energy in our physical bodies as well as our energetic bodies. In time, we can experience pain, tiredness, even exhaustion. Being aware of breathing and making a conscious choice to breathe more deeply is an enormous help in releasing stored emotional tension.

Exercise
Exercise is one thing I find very challenging to insert into a regular routine. However, I am totally committed to taking a brisk walk or dancing or something that is active when I feel I have emotion storing up that I'm not able to let go of through simple reflection or understanding. I am aware how this stored energy can build up and explode or implode if I don't find a way to release it.

Emotions
Often we have a somewhat limited array of emotions to choose from. In our post-industrial world where we were not allow
'feel', many of us have become numb to our f

emotions.

I remember many years ago when I was at university, going to see the counsellor. I have a vivid recollection of sitting on a bright green, vinyl bean bag and telling her that I was scared, that I didn't know what I felt anymore. I remember that she was a kind enough person but she wasn't able to help me at all. However, until we can identify our emotions accurately, we are not really able to release ourselves from them fully. When you're not sure how you feel, it can be useful to start with the question: "Am I sad, mad, scared or glad?" And then from there, refine the feeling. Otherwise something that is simply annoying can be given the label infuriating. Something dangerous can be misinterpreted as a bit scary. Something delightfully joyous can be undermined by 'good'. Once you know what you're experiencing, you can then manage the damage or embrace the wonder.

The following table is a great way to structure one's disturbing feelings and thinking to get some clarity and perspective in a way that is designed to help you make choices for moving forward.

How I feel	What triggered how I feel	How I'd like to feel	Easy achievable steps I need to take within 24 hours	Strengths that I know I have that will help me recover my dignity

Meditation

The a̶ of detaching from the chaos of your responsibilities, roles, r̶   ips, actions and feelings, gives you space and some   'o then return to your world with clarity and calm.

vou to recognise that emotions are not 'you'   e energies that have been set in motion,   s reactions mostly to external stimuli.

Meditation gives silent space to be able to recognise the distinction, letting go of the unconscious belief that 'I am my emotions and therefore what can I do?'

SQ

Meditation reconnects you to your original qualities/virtues. The act of being still, of learning to come to rest in the central core of your being, is the practice for true living – living in the state of being free from worry, free from disturbance, free from fear. Meditation also develops the Powers of the Shakti. Meditation reawakens your sense of your own eternity, the immortality of the 'soul' and the distinction from the form of matter...the body. This gives an enormous sense of security. Meditation re-forges the undeniable relationship between the Soul and the Supreme Soul. This relationship is exquisitely sweet, empowering and nurturing, loving and clarifying. It is like enabling the energetic construction of both a foundation and a backbone for the soul.

CQ

Meditation is essential for honing and aligning the creative powers of the mind and intellect to focus full energy on manifestation. Visualisation, affirmations, using the subtle region of the self to invoke into the material world, the magic of your own dreaming.

Being Present

Being in the 'now' is a true practice. The Buddhist practice of mindfulness is very helpful for being present. Being 'mindful' or consciously aware and focused at every moment, in every task, with every individual.

In Hinduism it is called Karma Yoga. Being present. In connection with the moment. Deep, unfettered listening to now.

EQ

Situations, reactions and emotions rule us when we are not present to them. However, when we stay present in the 'now', aware of our feelings, recognizing them as 'my' feelings, or reactions, not someone else's fault, they don't rule us as much. Name the feelings, write them down, map them out, run, walk, talk to yourself, before acting out. Wherever possible, don't act out the feelings until you've had a chance to understand them. But don't suppress them either. Being present enables you to stay with the feelings so as not to suppress, while being able to observe and therefore not associate as 'being' the feelings.

In this way it is also possible to say 'I am feeling angry, disappointed, a little frightened, upset, hurt, betrayed,' and so on. By saying 'I feel', it detaches you from actually 'being' the feeling. 'I feel angry', is better than 'I am angry', it says that there is a transitory process in play rather than an absolute identity.

If I feel something, I can observe and therefore be detached from the feeling more easily than I can do if I believe I am the experience. When we change the language we use, change our reality.

'I feel' is a better place to begin in relationship than "you are a ..." It is taking responsibility for how you feel rather than ascribing blame. When you take responsibility, you are stepping into a place of being powerful. When you ascribe blame, you are a victim, one who believes she is powerless to influence the situation.

SQ

Only in the 'now' are you able to connect to your own true self. Most of the time we are focused in the future or the past, involved in the unconscious activity of the mind's 60 000 thoughts a day. Being present is about being in the stillness of now.
- In that stillness, you find you.
- In that stillness you find your truth, your purpose, your

meaning and your way.

- In that stillness you can hear the voice of the divine whispering its guidance.
- In that stillness you see beyond the mundane to the magical.
- In that stillness you have access to all powers and all virtues.
- In that stillness there is no fear.
- In that stillness there is only a feeling of safety, of security.
- In that stillness your intuition is absolutely alive and clear.
- In that stillness there is you and God.
- From that stillness you become the creator of your world.

CQ

Being present ensures that ego stays out of the manifestation process. It means that you are able to see, hear, feel, taste, smell the subtle signals emerging from the play of life.

Being, you become the Master Weaver, awake to the all the threads of the creation that emerge, holding them, oiling the yarn, turning the wheel, waiting patiently as the weave and the wove come together to form the unfolding pattern.

In the now, without fear, you find the ease of moving into the future. Step by step, now moment by now moment, the future as you divine it unfolds.

The Detached Observer

This is the helicopter position, being on the balcony, imagining you are above, detached. It is a good practice to have to enhance your ability to observe yourself accurately. It also allows you to observe yourself in relation with others and to see the dynamics between you and another or within a group which is helpful for facilitating dialogue, recognising conflicting energies, seeing where you, the relationship or the group is stuck.

At whatever level we are working, this is a key state for EQ,

SQ and CQ.

EQ

The more we engage in a struggle with something, the less power we have in the situation. We become absorbed by the fight, and our perspective and perceptions narrow down to the orbit of the adversary. If we get absorbed by the 'problem' we drop ourselves into the same level and all our thinking and seeing is in relation to that. We are swimming in the soup of the tension and we are lost.

Managing our inner world, our emotional reactions, whether they be volatile or passively aggressive, it is crucial to maintain detachment from them. Not to be cut off or split from them, still responsible and aware, just not absorbed, owned or possessed by them. Not controlled by them.

SQ

At the same time, being detached from the roles that we play, not identifying as the teacher, as the mother, as the executive, as the helper, the star, the victim, the loser, the winner, as anything that is not intrinsic, gives us a greater ability to stay connected to our true selves.

As soon as you lose yourself in a role or a label and that role is in any way threatened, survival will govern your behavior and everything will move to align to survival.

The reality is of course that you continue long after you are no more an executive, or long after the children have grown up, or long after your boyfriend leaves you, or long after youth gives way to maturity. If we allow these roles to define us, then the roles will control us and we lose our security, ourselves and our spiri-tuality, any connection to meaning and purposeful living. We return to fear and competition and insecurity.

The detached observer – the first power of the Shakti – enables us to know first consciously, and later intuitively, which virtue or power is needed in any given situation to return us all and the system to harmony.

The Detached Observer, the Witness – Soul Consciousness – is the most profound tool of transformation.

In the awareness of the Detached Observer, I can connect with my subtle self, the light of consciousness that I am.

When I am in the awareness of light, I am a mere thought away from dancing in the light of the Divine. When I am one with God's light, then I am totally secure, full of beauty, love is a state of being rather than a feeling, and everything I see and feel is a reflection of this grace.

CQ

The Detached Observer enables us to recognize the signals, the coincidences, the creative patterns that are emerging in the process of manifestation.

Being detached from the outcome, we can then allow for the hand of the Divine to flow intrinsically into the manifestation. This ensures longevity, sustainability, beauty, natural development and evolution because we have not locked the creation into the limits of our own limited imagining.

The Detached Observer means we can perceive vast interconnecting webs of movement and it allows us to play our parts with humility, to make our contributions with joyful commitment, to enjoy the results without the anxiety or angst born of attachment.

Mirrors

This is the understanding that 'whatever is triggering emotion within me is just a mirror of something unseen in me'. Discern this and you begin the journey to becoming free from emotional reaction. This isn't always as simple as it might seem. Sometimes it is straightforward, for example, you get angry because someone is always late. Maybe you are also very often late or when you look at the underlying issue, you can see that you get annoyed when someone is late meeting you, because don't feel respected. Is there somewhere that you are not respecting another's values or time?

On one occasion, or rather in one relationship, it took me five years to finally be able to see in the mirror clearly. I would get closer with each viewing – the person is irresponsible, where am I irresponsible?

She doesn't get entangled in the burden of responsibility, maybe I am jealous because I wish I was free like that? All these things and others, helped me to see aspects of myself and to bring some valuable changes, but still I would get triggered by this individual. Finally, I came to understand it, but it was a 'blind spot', it was absolutely something that I couldn't see in myself.

Even when others who had the courage told me, I still couldn't see that it was a damaging or destructive thing. It wasn't until I was ready, until I was able to see without defensiveness that this was a trait in me that needed some discipline, that I finally became free.

Feeling controlled and tossed around by this woman's change-ability and lack of commitment, it never occurred to me that my continual 'inspiration for newness' was really the same and it caused a similar level of disturbance in others who were connected to my life and leadership. Now I am a little more cautious and hopefully somewhat more aware of my impact on others.

EQ

The use of 'mirrors' as an EQ tool is invaluable. It helps us to realize that there is no point to blame, it just makes us powerless victims.

Mirrors means taking responsibility for your own internal world and then noticing that when you do, your outer world, circumstances, relationships, also change. When I recognise that whatever triggers me in another, is something I can't see in myself, once I realize this absolutely, I become much more free from compulsive reaction to judge or blame others. It doesn't mean it stops completely and automatically. I need to own my reaction, look at what is triggering me, see where I can see that in my own actions and life. Once I do discover, then I am free and the miracle is that I don't react again ever in the same way.

SQ

In SQ you rely on the tool of 'mirrors' to see more clearly. The spiritual journey is about returning to beauty and to be able to see every smear on the glass of your own purity is profoundly helpful. You can go about cleaning and shining the diamond of the self. *Mirrors is always a gift in the domain of SQ.*

In the positive, if you are attracted to or impressed by anyone, Mirrors is a helpful tool so that you can see what it is that you are giving value to in someone else, but perhaps not owning in yourself. Anything seen in the mirror of another, is something unacknowledged in yourself. This is a wonderful disabler of jealousy and envy. If you admire something in another that would set you on a road to the green eyed demon of envy, all you need do is recognize that you have just been given a gift... the gift of seeing those qualities within yourself. Then the work begins to put energy, attention and power behind the intention to emerge them from the shadows.

CQ

If we are reacting, being drawn into anyone's qualities or defects, then we are being distracted from the flow of manifestation, from the living of our own lives. Quickly look in the mirror, clean it, clear the reaction, stop, be present and allow the river of life to continue to flow.

Mirrors helps us to keep our focus and attention in our creation rather than in the reaction to someone else's journey. It is a powerful and crucial tool in the realm of Creative Intelligence.

The 8 Powers

The 8 Powers are a way of looking at the subtle inner energies of transformation. They are a core teaching from the Brahma Kumaris World Spiritual University. (www.bkwsu.org).

These powers can be utilized anywhere on the spectrum from useful... supportive... empowering... transformational... to alchemical.

There is an in-depth exploration of each of the powers after this introduction.

EQ

All the 8 powers are helpful for self management and relationship management. They give order and structure to the invisible inner world, allowing you to see clearly different possibilities for responding to your emotional world.

For example, I love the Power to Tolerate and the Power to Accept as ways of being able to live with the emotions and not suppress or avoid them. Once Accepted, the power to Discern can identify what the emotion is, even what triggered it. The understanding of Mirrors or Projection is also a great tool here if there is someone else involved in the situation. Once Discerned, Decide what to do.

Finally the power to Face is without doubt, very useful. It enables you to move forward, confronting the demons within, allowing you to Cooperate with your own Decision and the support that will certainly come to you from the play of life.

SQ

These powers become the weapons of Shakti as you traverse the chasm between illusion and truth. They are the weapons you wield to extract yourself – your pure essence – from the Faces of survival, of illusion, the Traditional and Modern Faces.

The Shakti uses these powers to protect the innocence of her uncovered self, The Eternal Face. As you fire up these powers in the crucible of silence, they reveal themselves to you as invisible energies ready at your disposal for resolving, unearthing, redirecting, merging and emerging, unfolding, determining, liberating, experiencing.

In Spiritual Intelligence, the 8 Powers of the Shakti provide the fortress in which to establish the laboratory of your spiritual quest... your journey home to yourself and all your virtue, that is, to your innate beauty.

When used in alignment with the Divine, they are truly alchemical, transformational in nature. They liberate the survivor from her needs into one who is free and light, fulfilled and powerful.

CQ

Manifestation is a natural law, a way of moving through life from a spontaneous state of thought into action into form. The loss of true identity birthed the survival Faces and these Faces are fear-based, which prohibits the natural flow of the creative process.

When Shakti forms a union with the Divine as Shiv-Shakti, you are able to ignite the purification role of these Powers to clear the patterns of fear and insecurity in the soul that would divert, deter or undermine creation. Then these Powers are God's powers which you claim as your right, as you manifest your way into the light and harmony of your own personal paradise.

THE 8 POWERS OF THE SHAKTI

withdraw
Know when to step back - detach from the role, the situation... get perspective.

co-operate
Surrender ego and force.
Lend your talents to others and to circumstances - read the omens and flow with them.

let go
From yourself from the chains of the past... when it's over, finish it and move on.

face
The courage and strength to handle whatever happens, whatever you feel, whatever you see... inside and out.

tolerate
Go beyond the insistence of reaction. Rise above... seek the wisdom of understanding.

decide
The power to take action, to commit and follow the course you know is right.

accept
Leave behind the fantasy of 'should': work with the truth of 'what is'.

discern
The power to see what's really going on, to clearly assess what's true from what's not.

Introducing The 8 Powers

These 8 Powers are ours. The role of Shakti is a leadership role no matter where you are in your life. If you are working in a supermarket at the check-out, you can influence the lives of thousands of people with your attitude, your powers and virtues. You can take the lead in transforming people's days, relationships and lives by your interaction with them, by the energy that you transmit, by the way that you 'look' at them.

In the same way, if you are a mother, a teacher, a student, a manager, a scientist, a television presenter, president of a country or an organization, you have the power to lead, to lead people out of the limited experience that we have somehow agreed is acceptable.

The 8 powers of the Shakti's leadership are outlined in the pages that follow.

Working with the 8 Powers

There are five ways of increasing and enhancing these powers in your life.

The first is simply to know that you have them, that they are your birthright.

The second is to contemplate the powers. Think deeply about them and what they mean and how they can work for you in your life. Understand the nuances of each one and how they help you see your life and situations in new ways, allowing for more harmony and magic in your world.

The third is to practice using them. Like anything, the more that you use them, the more they become a powerful art form, transforming your world. However, it is important to practice using them in situations that don't require mastery level.

There's no point trying to wield the Power to Tolerate for the first time in your life, when your mother with whom you have always had a difficult relationship, comes to stay for a month. Practice tolerating while someone is abusive in traffic, or when your partner is doing that thing that drives you a bit crazy, or when the kids just won't eat their dinner.

The fourth method is to flame them in the fire of meditation.

The very act of turning within, connecting to your own source of inner strength, helps you to become aware of these subtle powers and to grow this energy.

The fifth and most powerful, is to draw those powers from the Source of all power. Tuning into your own form of light, you can then tune into the frequency of God's Divine Light, bringing extra energy/power into yourself.

When connecting with the Supreme Source, these are very real and practical powers that are accessed. These powers help define and protect the way forward. They enable you to do transformational work within yourself and within in the world. In recognizing that the external is a direct correlate of the internal, these powers bring light and clarity and strength to the first point of creation... the inner world.

When the outer world is confused, the Shakti clears the path by turning inward and clearing the chaos within.

These 8 Powers are foundational tools for transformation of the self in action and as such, transformation of our world.

WAYS OF RELATING TO THE 8 POWERS

In this chapter, you will find that there are a number of ways of relating to the Powers. This is very specifically designed to support you in the way that you best learn, remember, integrate and are inspired.

The Colours
Through meditation, a long time yogi and colour therapist, sat with each of the powers and arrived at the corresponding colours. Colours are simply expressions of different energies or frequencies in the same way as are ideas, thoughts, feelings. If colours work for you, use these colours to awaken your remembering of your powers. Wear the colours, visualise the colours, decorate with the colours. Whatever works to remind you of the Powers that you have. You will find the colour wheel on the website www.fourfacesofwoman.com .

The Image
There are images using the same colours which have metaphorical relationship to each power. For some, it is easier to remember an image than a concept.

The Reflection
There is a short metaphor connecting the power with the image.

The Story
From simple real life situations, to support your practical and intuitive understanding of each power. You may notice that each story has a number of different powers merged within it, however I have highlighted just one in each story.

The Wisdom
For those who want to go deeper. If this is you, I suggest that you

write more about each power, coming from your own thinking, feeling, perceiving. Writing is a great way of turning someone else's ideas into your own.

The Archetypes
Using 8 Goddesses (known as Shaktis) from an eastern tradition, you can work with the energy of these archetypes to shift consciousness. Take on the identities when you need to rise to that transformational power.

You may like to seek out images from other traditions or cultures that relate more to you and your journey. At one point I bought myself a small statue of Kuan Yin, the female form of the Buddha. It was useful for me in my quest to be more compassionate, as she is the archetypal representation of compassion.

In recent years as I've been working with love. I opened my car one day and there was a small silver medal of the Virgin Mary on the driver's side floor. I have absolutely no idea how she came to be there, but I have kept her in my wallet as a reminder of developing unconditional love.

The Distortion
This is simply to highlight that because these powers are resources of the soul, they exist always and are therefore used by the survival Faces – Traditional and Modern – in distorted form. Examples of these distortions are included so that there can be clarity about using them.

The Virtues
There are four key qualities – virtues – that link to each power. Focus on bringing those virtues into your attitude and behavior, helps to anchor the power into your being.

A Bit of Advice...

Discerning the Power

As you read about the powers, they may seem too absolute, even unattainable. And because these are powers, they are indeed absolute, they are pure and potent. If they are mixed with the consciousness of the Traditional or Modern faces, they are distorted manipulations of the powers. But relax...we are bound to do this because this *is* what we do to survive. At the same time, by raising our conscious awareness now, is the time when we can purify our powers, using them more and more as they really are. So when we 'hit the mark' with the powers, they will act to totally transform a feeling, a situation. When we don't hit the mark, it is not bad or wrong, we will simply know because the situation will not be fully resolved.

Accumulating the Power

The aim is to develop the mastery around these powers, just as we would with any skill set. Focus, Practice then Become. Even a little attention brings profound results. The 8 Powers becoming incredible tools that you can wield at will to empower your life and choices and to be of service to others and the world. And when you experience the successes, it is important to acknowledge them, realise they came from your use of these powers. This helps accumulate the powers and encourages you to continue develop them.

Honouring the Power

Being grateful too is a helpful way of keeping the ego at bay, of remaining humble whilst being powerful. In fact, the more you gain mastery of the powers, the more authority you amass, ironically the more humble you will find yourself being. You won't have to prove anything, you will find yourself sitting in strength and you will simply be profoundly grateful for having been guided back to your source by the Source.

The Power to Withdraw

THE REFLECTION

There are times in life when I need to withdraw my energy from a situation. Sometimes I can step back in my mind, ... be on the balcony, observing everyone.... even myself... and then there are other times when I need to walk away, to leave the scene altogether.

I think of how it must be for an astronaut, one who sees planet earth for the first time from space. Totally withdrawn...such a different perspective.

THE STORY

During a retreat few years ago, a young woman stayed behind in a tea break to speak with me. She was a little disturbed and wanted to know if I could help. This is always a little daunting because some of the stories that people tell of their lives, I'm not at all qualified to give advice about. This young woman was no exception.

At these times, my practice is to be very silent internally with no thoughts, just listening in stillness, waiting for some inspiration and the 'right' thing to show up in my intellect.

This is the first aspect of Power to Withdraw... to be able to step back from any sense of self other than the quiet consciousness within, to detach from roles, responsibilities, beliefs, relation-ships. To be the observer, without judgement or opinion.

So there I was, exercising the Power to Withdraw as Chloe explained her dilemma.

"Have you ever heard of walk-ins?" she asked me.

"I don't know, explain a little more," I said, waiting for some context to what she was asking.

She explained that she believed herself to be a 'walk-in'. She shared that in her belief, this time of change that the world is in, requires a lot of individual souls to do their job, to fulfil their purposes, quickly. Because of the need for speed, there isn't the time for souls to be born and grow to adulthood in the normal manner. Apparently, this means that some souls take over adult bodies from another soul and that one body could have a number of souls coming and going in sequence over time, using it to deliver their gift to humanity.

Now this is not at all part of my framework of understanding, but I can't say by any means that it is wrong. Really how would I know? What I did find, was that Chloe was incredibly sincere and earnest in her desire to find the answer to her question. If I had been with her and been locked into my different 'beliefs', then I would not have been able to help her. But to be silent, withdraw from myself as 'Caroline', connect with God and then listen, meant I was able to feel a way forward for her that was a genuinely sound piece of advice that neither disregarded her story, nor compromised my personal integrity.

"What happens when the time comes, when I've fulfilled my purpose and I have to leave this body for another 'walk-in' to take over?"

I remember being so silent within. I wanted to be available for the 'right' answer that would offer her a way forward, knowing that my wisdom is limited. And so in the silence I connected to God and waited. Then I knew.

I told Chloe that her question was exactly the same question that sits at the heart of my practice too – how to be so free to leave when it is time. That the art of Raja Yoga meditation is to deeply know the distinction between the 'self' and the body... at an experiential level, not just intellectually. Any of us needs to be ready to move on at any time. We don't know what will happen today, tomorrow, next week. When Michael, my husband died, the doctor thought he would last another two months more. I had told him only 36 hours earlier, after months of trying to save him, that if it was his time to go, then I would be fine and he could leave in peace. And that is what he did. Once the body became very difficult to live in, the soul withdrew its energy and let go of any attachment he had to the life of Michael. This is the final aspect of the Power to Withdraw.

To be able to Withdraw absolutely whether from the beliefs and structure of ego identities, from a situation that is destructive or limiting or from the body ... the practice is the same.

Soul Consciousness. I am not this body. I am a soul, a point of light. Pure in essence. Full in energy. Divine. A tiny invisible star of pure consciousness, so small it is impossible to see. I live in this body, work in partnership with this body, extending my life force throughout the body, but I am energy.

The deep practice throughout the day of remembering this, makes the Power to Withdraw very accessible and also makes your meditation very easy, beautiful and empowering. And so Chloe went to take her morning tea feeling deeply satisfied. I felt deeply grateful for this Power that let me be true to her and to myself.

THE WISDOM

The Power to Withdraw is about perspective. It gives clarity and coolness, as well as the ability to change a situation. To withdraw is to detach or step back from whatever the current situation is – feelings, emotions, confusion, interaction – whatever my potential reactions might be, the insistence of outward situations that seek to draw me into their webs.

This power is fundamental to transformation and the Shakti's leadership, where moving forward into domains of unmapped futures requires detachment from old patterns of thinking, being and reacting.

To Withdraw, it is critical to understand that we are actors, playing roles, players in the game. If we begin to believe the game, to become caught in the identity of the role, we lose power to create, to contribute, to be free to shape new paths. As soon as we merge into the role, we become attached to everything associated with that identity.

The awareness of being the actor keeps us free from the insistence of tradition and conservatism. The Power to Withdraw also ensures that we have access to other powers crucial to the journey. When there is no map for the future, when we are truly rewriting the fundamentals of the way we live and work, we must be entirely creative... purely creative... Not minor adjustments, not incremental change, but quantum leaps are required. Quantum leaps in creative thinking and manifestation are born from a free mind, a still and silent inner world that becomes the receptacle for genius.

This is the alchemy of the Shakti. The way to this instrumental power is through meditation and simply learning to make my mind quiet. Speak less... think less. Grow a discipline within the self.

The Power to Withdraw also tells us when it is time to leave a scene, a situation, a role. It is the power to walk away when the time of leaving has arrived. The Power to Withdraw underpins and works as the pivot for the Power to Discern.

THE ARCHETYPE
Shakti / Goddess Parvati

The Shakti is directly connected with the Supreme Source of all and in this power, the archetype is represented by Parvati. She is the wife of Shiva, but her story is of independence. Whilst Shiva was in the mountains performing austerities as a way of grieving the death of his previous wife Santi, Parvati began her own retreat. Through isolation, introspection and deep meditation, she became independently powerful. It was her detachment from the physical world and its relationships that allowed her to tap the fountain of divine power.

The Power to Withdraw does not require one to leave the world and live out life in the barren mountains, but rather empowers the Shakti with the same sense of detachment whilst living fully in the physical world.

The rosary symbolises Parvati's Power to Withdraw. Whilst being threaded, connected with many other beads, she remains independent and clear in her singular identity. The fact that she is accompanied by the life-giving 'sacred cows' indicates that her powers are sacred and that the energy she accumulates and shares is life-giving.

THE DISTORTION

When used through the consciousness of Modern or Traditional Face, this becomes a manipulation for control rather than a power from a divine source. It becomes manipulative to shut down, to withhold our energy, or cut off our contribution, withdraw from communication. This is an old powerless way of trying to get power from others.

Rather than cutting off from another who in your relationship appears to have 'won the power', it is better to Withdraw from your own pattern and observe without judgement that you are using this manipulation. As soon as you move into observation, you become a little more detached and are able to regain power. After that, you can see which power or virtue you use next to move forward.

THE VIRTUES

Silence
Detachment
Introspection
Concentration

THE COLOUR - Ocean Blue

The Power to Let Go

THE REFLECTION

The past can feel like chains, binding me tightly to things that are
no longer successful, relevant or helpful. If it is true that most of
my thoughts are in some way or another about the past... and if it
is true that my future is created by my thoughts... then unless I
stop this wasteful thinking, I am bound to create the past again.

*So let me do something... let go of these thoughts... let them float up
and far away... and the further they go, the lighter I feel... and the
further they go, the quieter my mind becomes.*

THE STORY

I met Norma at a retreat in France. It was a retreat on the Fifth
Face. The Fifth Face is completely dedicated to practical, personal
experimentation of the relationship between each one and God,
the Divine. Ann came with her two friends. As it turned out,
neither Norma nor the friend who brought her along believed in
God at all. Norma was enraged with God, so actually she did
believe. During the course of the weekend, she became angrier
and angrier. Some time on Saturday afternoon her friend Decided
not to participate in the retreat any longer, rather to spend the
time in the beautiful environment in her own space. She too was
feeling angry. It was a good thing. As we shared with each other

at the end of the retreat, it allowed Norma to find her own journey rather than be caught in her friend's story.

So there was Norma with her bad back, she managed herself by bringing a collapsible lounge and cushions so that she could lie down throughout the workshop. Upon reflection, it was truly a remarkable power within the soul to make such an effort to engage with such a volatile theme, in such discomfort.

As it transpired, we came to understand Norma's anger. Twenty years earlier her baby daughter had died. She was only one year old. Since that time, she had refused to allow the light of God into her life because she blamed 'Him' for her pain and loss. She had been unable to hear, see, feel anything other than that pain and it blinded her. Somehow, immersed in the silence and reflection and good company and nourishing food of that weekend, she was able to see.

The Power to Withdraw is the fundamental first step and then Let Go. Throughout this weekend, Norma participated in many activities that utilised the Power to Withdraw. As the journey continued, she was more and more open, and hopeful, I think, to understanding the past, to recognising the cause, to seeing her life today not through the filter of that loss.

Many of the exercises we do in the Fifth Face are practical experiments in connecting with the energy of God and bringing that energy, directing as a gift into the world. Norma had this experience and she was able to realize who God really is, that God doesn't have anything to do with life and death and accidents and illness or good fortune. That the world we create is based on our own thinking and actions, and that the results are not always experienced in one lifetime, they can be carried forward. Somehow after twenty years of deep pain, Norma was able to see through the fog, and could see it was time to Let Go of the past, the beliefs that kept her impoverished in her own spirit and in relationship with God and also, in terms of her sense of purpose and destiny.

About a week after the retreat, I received a letter from Norma's friend – the atheist, who was working through her own resistance with great letting go and courage. She said that Norma had left the retreat committed to being a channel for God's energy in the world, that there were three people in her life who were dying and she knew that she could give this gift of pure, divine energy to each soul to help them on their journey. She was at peace, filled with purpose and powerful in her connection to the present and herself.

THE WISDOM

This is the power to cut away everything that is destructive, useless and wasteful. It is the power to be free and to hold nothing of the past in your heart, or anything pointless of the future in your mind. It is the strength to say 'No' to negativity. Letting go requires courage, forgiveness, trust and purity. It means my life starts anew from this moment onwards.

It helps one to Let Go of all limitations of identity. It means finishing in your mind what others expect of you and what you expect of others. Letting Go of limited thinking and beliefs and identity. Letting Go of any attachment to an existing way, being prepared to allow something utterly new to emerge. When you Let Go of the expectations you have of yourself based on what others/society expect, then you can have greater understanding and compassion not only for yourself but also for others. This is crucial in the role of the leader. In Letting Go of the burden of expectations, one is free to make decisions that are incisive and imbued with the power of truth rather than the force of tradition. In holding a vision of a new way of living and working together, this power compels you to finish attachments to the current ways. It leaves you able to Let Go of the ego's attraction to position. To go beyond the opinions of others, and Let Go of 'what I think I know and who I think I am'.   Then I see anew.

THE ARCHETYPE
Shakti / Goddess Durga

Durga is the archetype for the Power to Let Go. She is worshipped as the destroyer of defects. Anything that isn't pure and true, she destroys, using knowledge and detachment. Her symbols are many. Her main weapon in this context is the Sword of Illusion. The sword symbolises the power of knowledge to cut away all that is illusory, all that is limited.

Durga is the one in mythology who defeated the great demon Mahishma, freeing the world of evil. The Power to Let Go is the power to Let Go of the dark which we cling to from habit and from want of knowing better. It is the power that enables us to take hold of the light.

When women can collectively use this power to 'finish' history and the way that history has shaped their character, the world can change. Whilst we carry in our psyche the imprint of degradation and subservience, we will either submit or react – neither of which brings about a new, a better way.

THE DISTORTION

When used through the consciousness of Traditional and Modern Faces, this power distorts and becomes denial and suppression, not dealing with issues or feelings that will certainly sabotage you in my efforts. Denial and suppression are not Letting Go, they are not powers, rather they are simply survival strategies for dealing with situations and feelings that are overwhelming. Letting Go lets us acknowledge these thoughts and feelings as unhelpful or damaging, and then make a conscious choice as to what to do with them.

THE VIRTUES

Self Respect
Discipline
Postiveness
Purity

THE COLOUR - Violet

The Power to Tolerate

THE REFLECTION

Nothing in life is perfect. Sometimes things aren't at all how I like them to be and sometimes I end up in the path of someone else's negative energy.

But if I want to remain strong and happy, I can't afford to react to anything. I can't afford to take anything personally.

A tree will give shade and rest even to someone who carves into it is trunk. In the same way, I have to be beyond insult. When a storm attacks the tree, the tree doesn't fight back... it doesn't take the storm personally. It bends and sways, and the storm passes.

THE STORY

When I was growing up, my father and I clashed enormously. We were very, very different. Today we have more in common as we have traveled our own, yet often intersecting spiritual paths. But we are still fundamentally different in the way in which we see and approach the management of life.

I always found myself either trying to get my father's approval. Or, on the other side, presuming that I would never get it, I would rebel and do things that would attract his disdain or anger. Looking back, I understand it was simply another way of getting his attention – but it wasn't a positive way to go about it, either for him or for me.

My father had gone into business with my sister Donna in the early 1990s and they made quite a success the sale of some software products and in the eventual sale business itself. In his younger days, my father had been successful in starting a manufacturing business with almost no money, then he had built it to a point where he sold it for a handsome profit.

When I started my business in 1997, and got my first big contract with a major bank in 1998, I think I felt I had made it with my father. He was indeed pleased. This contract lasted nine months and I employed eight other people, everything looked set to be a success for me, and my father.

Unfortunately not so. I hadn't learned that you have to work both in the business and on the business, meaning that while you are doing the work you have to be looking for more work and building the infrastructure of the business. After many months of no work, and many conversations where my father challenged what I was doing, I finally had a conversation with him that changed my life forever.

On this particular day we were talking on the phone and I was explaining to my father my strategy for getting business. It was a creative strategy, inviting people to a breakfast where we showcased our transformative theatre process. It required a small investment but I thought it was worth it. At that stage, we'd had four breakfasts and while there was hugely positive feedback, there was no business coming in. My father is from the old school of sales people that say 'just keep knocking on doors'.

So there we were on the phone this day. "Basil, I worry about you. I don't know how you can survive running a business in that way." (Yes, my father calls me Basil!)

Under normal circumstances, for the previous 39 years, I would have reacted emotionally. This day, something was different. After years of meditation, of practicing soul conscious detachment, I found there was no emotion rising up to do battle.

All was quiet. Then I heard myself, my voice, very calmly speaking to Kev, my father.

"Dad...do you believe in the power of thought?"

"Well, yeah, of course, you know I do, Basil."

"Now Dad, I understand that your worry is coming from care and concern. However, I don't know if you realize that your doubt is polluting my dream. If you can, it would be much better and more helpful for me if you could turn your worry into faith."

A moment's silence from Kev. "Yep...alright Basil. I can do that."

A few minutes later we hung up the phone happily. My father went off to London to visit my brother the next day and when he returned five weeks later, I had a call from him. I was on business interstate where he lived and was just going into a meeting.

"Your sister tells me you've managed to get some new business while I've been away?"

You can imagine the jubilation I was feeling. In just five weeks, since our last conversation, having signed three large contracts. So there I was on my mobile phone, outside my client's office and I said to my father...

"That's right Dad. And you know what?

"No, what?"

"I didn't have to knock on even one door!"

He paused a moment then said, "There you go Basil...that's the power of my faith!"

I laughed. Why not, I thought. After years of reacting and taking things far too personally, and after years of practicing meditation, growing these powers, I was able to use the right power at the right time. The Power to Tolerate allowed both of us to be free. Not only that, but my father was able to use his thoughts to support me and to see a tangible result from the power of faith. This is life-changing stuff. For me, I was liberated from a lifetime of feeling insecure, disapproved of, not good enough, in my relationship with my father.

Today, we occasionally have some interference in our relationship, but nothing like it used to be and certainly we don't react from pain in the ways that we used to do. We are able to speak openly with love to each other – often initiated by him – and the healing that takes place is immediate and kind and resonates throughout time. Both of us feel very blessed to share the journey of life together.

THE WISDOM

The path of a spiritual transformation is not the path of ease, though it is often confused with such. There are many things to Tolerate. You have to Tolerate your own inadequacies, your doubts, lack of clarity and the shadows that you start to perceive as you grow your light.

In addition, all of us live in relationship with others within systems of energetic dependency, reacting off each other, struggling for power. We do that struggle differently, whether as a perfectionistic tyrant, an interrogator/inquisitor, a victim, an isolationist, or various other forms of manipulating power.

When you begin to change, and the people around you feel you changing and becoming detached from the energy system of dependency, their unconscious discomfort causes them to react, project and blame those they believe responsible for their discomfort. This is rarely rational, but when people feel threatened, they resort to survival tactics.

The Power to Tolerate is the power to handle whatever anyone doles out. It is the power to see beyond the behavior, recognizing and then dealing with the motivation that drives the behavior.

People are all in energetic systems of relationship, especially those with whom we are close, but bear in mind that even strangers who abuse you on the freeway are simply trying to 'win' energy from someone else because they feel they are without resources to deal with whatever is happening in their lives.

The Power to Tolerate knows compassion and uses it wisely. It is the power to find understanding and kindness for the person while using the Power to Face to deal with their unacceptable actions – even if that person is myself.

In its most profound form, the Power to Tolerate enables the Shakti to lead another person, group or system to a different state, by not buying into the power games of abuse or manipulation, but by being able to understand the deepest need within the soul and then giving that energy where it is needed.

So if someone is hurt and projecting anger from their pain, the Shakti can transform the anger with the balm of compassion and comfort, sharing that vibration or feeling with the other.

The Power to Tolerate means nothing is personal and it means one can access deep insight and maturity. At the very essence, you find a well of unconditional Love.

THE ARCHETYPE
Goddess / Shakti Jagadamba

Jagadamba – the Great World Mother is the archetype for this power.

It is said that there is no need to Tolerate if there is unconditional love.

Tolerance starts with being the mother to myself, tolerating my inconsistencies, failings, and seeing past all the limitations in order to love myself, the pure soul completely. When I can Tolerate my own limitations, I am more able to do that for others.

Jagadamba carries the most weapons of all the Shaktis,

symbolizing how much power is truly needed to Tolerate and to love fully, with a pure heart, without desire for return and without conditions.

Jagadamba as the World Mother embraces all the people of the world as her children, understanding that bad behavior is only born of fear and insecurity.

Her connection with the Ocean of Love, God as the Mother, is so overwhelming that she is able to continually love beyond the fear. She can Tolerate all things, though she does not ever allow her own dignity to diminish.

In this role, wielding this Power, the Shakti is the Protector of Innocence – in the self and others. As Mother she will do whatever it takes to keep her innocent children safe and this is an unassailable force. She is the one who keeps our world from total corruption and it is through her love and Tolerance that the world is restored to right values.

THE DISTORTION

When filtered through the Traditional or Modern Faces, the power to Tolerate becomes distorted, so that the woman plays the role of the self sacrificing martyr. The martyr role can feel extremely noble, but no matter which way you look at it, it is still a way of manipulating energy to win the game of feeling worthwhile and worthy, and/or getting attention, energy, power.

THE VIRTUES

Understanding
Patience
Acceptance
Fearlessness

THE COLOUR - Magenta

The Power to Accept

THE MEDITATION

So much pain happens because I hold fast to what 'should be' ... my ego's unwillingness to accept 'what is'.

Yet dealing with reality makes sense.

Accepting 'what is'... then listening for what's next.

Releasing control.

Learning to trust.

And as I flow naturally through the twists and turns of this journey... life becomes as easy as a river finding its way to the ocean.

THE STORY

In 2005 I went to Poland. There I met some great women including one woman I will call Anita. Anita is a journalist and film maker, who is now in her sixties and so is not really employable in the current capitalist regime of Poland. Although communism was not a pleasant system by any stretch of the imagination, from what she told me, for her it was a better – or rather more secure – world.

So here she was, an intelligent, beautiful woman, disempowered by the system that had made her feel safe. It hadn't given her the security that she really wanted at all, it had simply made her dependent on it.

During a weekend retreat of the Four Faces in Warsaw, we were doing an exercise with the 8 Powers. I often take with me a giant fabric colour wheel that is placed on the floor. It resembles the one in the chapter on the Eight Powers of the Shakti. However, it doesn't have any identification as to which colour relates with which power. I ask the women to close their eyes, to tune into but not become absorbed by an unresolved question in their lives, either at the conscious or unconscious level. Then when they have it in their mind, I ask them to open their eyes and move toward the wheel, walking over all colours until stopping on the one that most draws them.

Only after they choose their one colour, do I tell them which colour represents which power. I also tell them the story of the Shakti or Goddess that relates to each one. This is a strikingly effective use of intuition. The coincidences, realizations and 'ahas' that emerge from the session are often remarkable.

So after I told Anita that by standing on the turquoise she had chosen the Power to Accept, she was incensed. There was no way that she was going to agree to this. She felt she had been tricked, that really she should have chosen Discern or Face or even Tolerate... but Accept? – Never!

I asked her to just wait and let's see how things turn out. On another day Antia will likely choose another colour, but on that day, it was Acceptance. She went off into her group of other 'Acceptees' to talk about their chosen power for that day.

So after the groups had had their time to share, I asked them to come back into the large group. Anita was still not exactly happy about her choice. We did our group meditation. I have no idea of the meditation commentary that I spoke, but after it was over and everyone had opened their eyes, it was as if I was looking at a completely different woman. Anita was quiet and gently contained. Her face was serene... and sublimely so. Her eyes were truly like deep pools of peace.

We continued with the workshop until the tea break. When the group dispersed outside, I entered the tranquil aura of the waiting Anita. "What happened?" I asked.

It seemed that in the meditation, Anita had been transported to a garden where there was a tiny hut. As she described the hut and the man who was in the garden outside the hut, I recognized that she was talking about a place I got to regularly on retreat in Mt Abu in India. Anita had never been there herself and yet she had had a vision of the place and the man who had founded the Brahma Kumaris World Spiritual University.

Anita shared her 'vision'. She was together with this man, Brahma Baba as he is known, in the garden, he was smiling with great love and carrying in his arms a beautiful bunch of turquoise lilies. Of course in dreams and meditations, the unreal becomes very real and so there can be such things as turquoise lillies.

"They're beautiful," she had said to him.

"They are aren't they," he agreed. "They are for you." He held them out, offering them to her with so much love, and as she went to take them, he said, "So why won't you accept life?"

She told us at that very moment, something melted in her... the resistance to life as it had become. The fear and complaints and insecurities all just faded as she Accepted the flowers.

Before I left Poland, I saw Anita a couple more times. I don't know how she is these days, but as the time passed during my visit in Warsaw, I watched her grow stronger and more beautiful and more in peace. The Power to Accept gifted her a resounding contentment and from that space, she started to create her life.

THE WISDOM

This is the power that delivers peace and contentment to our lives. It requires humility – an understanding that we don't know the whole story and that there is often a better way that will emerge if we can allow it to do so.

If the vision of a more sustainable future is powerful enough within you, then you will attract all that is required to manifest that future. It won't always be the manifestation that you expect it to be; indeed it can seem contrary to your plan. At this time, just Accepting without judgment offers a new window into the journey. At this point, you don't need to control, or judge or fix or change... just need to rest the ego and Accept 'what is'. Even if the situation seems dire, understand that once you have Accepted it, there will be peace in your mind, heart and relationships and this peace will give birth to a creative path forward, bringing with it new energy and renewed commitment.

This is also the power to move into the world without having to judge or assess all that you encounter. It is the power of innocence, of allowing all to be as they are, and of understanding that what you might mark as good or bad, right or wrong, comes from conditioning and not from truth. The world is full of vast difference. Not better, not worse... just different.

When each of us is authentic, true to who we are, the need to compare is no longer relevant. We find ourselves totally at peace and able to be at peace with others, flowing through life and finding that life supports us in our endeavours.

If we think of contentment and happiness as treasures that are so worthwhile that they need to be guarded and cared for, then the Power to Accept is a the protector of your contentment.

THE ARCHETYPE
Goddess / Shakti Santoshima

Santoshima is the Goddess of Contentment and is the archetype who is connected to the Power to Accept. She carries the trident, destroying all preferences and opinions based on ego, greed and attachment. She also carries the Sword of Illusion and a bowl of rice. The bowl of rice represents the idea that all the grains are different and yet with each one accepted as part of the offering, there is a sense of wholeness, of nourishment and nurture, of tranquillity and non-violence.

THE DISTORTION

When acting from the survival faces of Tradition and Modernity, the Power to Accept becomes a self-destructive option. Traditional Face Accepts things just to keep the peace, because it is easier, to maintain external harmony, but it means compromising our dignity and shutting out our voice of inner knowing. In Accepting in this way, we undermine our self-worth and self-respect.

The Modern Face compromises by Accepting that which appears to be opposite to the tradition she renounced. It might not be what she wants, but she uses it as an escape from what she doesn't want.

THE VIRTUES

Flexibility
Openness
Mercy
Gentleness

THE COLOUR - Turquoise

The Power to Discern

THE REFLECTION

To clearly see what's true from what's not, and to know what's really going on, I have to step back. Detaching from my opinions and from the situation, I perceive much more clearly.

Strangely, this stepping back acts like a magnifying glass. Bringing together detachment and focus, I see the whole story and all its parts... and I can understand the truth of the moment. I feel clear and certain.

THE STORY

This is one of my stories. It was the worst and the best year of my life. The worst, because it undid everything about me. Whatever made me feel secure was ripped away. The best, because I found myself, heightened my subtle resources such as discernment and intuition, learned to trust myself and life, began to undo the workaholic style existence I'd been living, I became self-reliant, started tapping into my creativity, glimpsed the future, started to learn a new way of manifesting, found a more stable sense of security, and most jubilantly, initiated the funeral for the victim within.

It was 1999. I was on retreat in India. I had been there about a week, when I realized that I felt different than I had ever felt in my life. Profound, deep, abiding peace. Never before had I realized how peaceless I was. What had happened? Why did I feel so incredibly quiet and still and gentle? Then I recognized that I had not had a single thought about the future for maybe two days. I had not generated one single idea in that time! For me that was a record. It was January and I took this experience to be a signal for the year ahead. I committed to staying in the present, to not think about the future for the whole year.

Things started out well. While in India, I received an email from Mauritius asking me to go there for International Women's Day and run a Four Faces program. Great! I thought, an exotic start to the year. I was living in a house which I believed to be a long-term arrangement, so when I arrived back from India to Australia, I found a new office space, we redecorated and it was fantastic. We auditioned for actors and facilitators to work with us in our budding consultancy, working with transformation in organizations. I hired another person to help me with marketing and off the year went.

Sorry, not so fast! As we moved into the office, spent a month or so renovating, I still didn't have any work on the horizon. I wasn't worried, I had a strategy and a huge public success just behind me. All would be well. And besides, I was in my commitment not to think about the future. Naturally I did do some planning for the business but I was restricting myself to do-able planning not 'dreaming' ideas.

As the weeks became months and no work appeared, the bank balance dropped, despite all my marketing efforts, And there I was 'stuck' in the present, feeling all the uncomfortable feelings I had previously escaped by living in the future.

I realised how insecure I felt. In the past, I had lived off the strategy that no matter how dire today might look, tomorrow was always bright and shiny, in my mind anyway. Basically, I had been living in a fantasy. But now according to my commitment, there I was abandoned to the present reality of insecurity, vulnerability and financial challenge. Furthermore, the house was about to be sold and I would have to find somewhere else to live – not a drama if you have plenty of cash, but it was now November and I had none. Everything started to fall around me.

Perhaps the worst thing was that I had so long been out of the 'present' I didn't have a real sense of myself. Rather I lived in a slightly fantasized version of me, and that version was pretty okay. However, there's no escaping the fact that when you start to live in the 'now', in the present time, you are confronted with yourself. Not your true, original self, but the unconscious survival patterns of the egoic self. So I was insecure, vulnerable, close to destitute and seeing my dysfunctionality close up and personal perhaps for the first time ever.

The relationships in my life became a reflection of my own state and I felt very alone. Naturally the victim character pranced onto the stage for a showy encore.

Yet ever so slowly my commitment started to pay off. I was learning to Tolerate feeling this discomfort, to a much greater extent than I had before.

I was seeing, Discerning, very clearly in a way I had never been able to in the past. It was as if the invisible dynamics made themselves obvious to me. I could see strings and patterns that wound around people and ideas and things. I could see my own modes of survival behavior as distinct from my real self.

And I was starting to be able to Discern the future. This was very different from visioning, planning or determining. This was about glimpsing. Windows were opening to show me what lay ahead. Not the whole picture. At first when I would see something I would swing into action, trying to wrap strategies and plans around what I had seen, but they didn't work. Later I realized that I wasn't supposed to do anything, I was just supposed to hold the window open and stay alert.

As time went on, as things started unblock and work flowed, I flowed and life unfolded, I began to Discern people, situations and even commercial services that had the same 'resonance' as the future windows I had seen.

But being a part of a bigger plan rather than being a planning addict, you have to be patient. Yes, it is possible to construct and control a whole lot of things, but when you do, you miss the magic.

The Power to Discern is a beautiful key to unlocking the appearance of magic in your life. And while magic exists always as certainly as you do, it is the Power to Discern that allows you to capture the wonder, seeing it with a divine vision, a third eye. Then your security becomes anchored in the quality of your thoughts and actions today. You realise that tomorrow doesn't exist in your mind, tomorrow is a consequence of the alignment of virtues and actions that happen today.

So even though I learned through a 'trial by fire' approach, it was one of the most valuable, multi-results lessons I've learned on this path. And I found out that it is only possible to truly see, to really Discern, when you are detached and observing the survivor self while firmly planted in the present. Yes, you glimpse the future and you carry the relevance of the past, but you live in the now – listening, alert, attentive and available.

THE WISDOM

This is the power of using the higher intellect. It is the art of consulting the most conscient self to understand the knowledge of truth and falsehood, right and wrong, reality and illusion, benefit and loss.

Using this power the Shakti is able to Discern accurately. It is the power of clarity, to see with different eyes, hear with different ears. The power to Discern is about trusting our highest selves even in the face of opposing opinions, or outdated but active beliefs. It is the power to listen to what is known deep within.

It is the power to hold still and look for the truth of the moment before reacting. Reaction is the course of being controlled by external stimuli – a state of powerlessness. The

Power to Discern is like a window that allows the Shakti to step out of compulsive reactions, and as an observer, see the reality of the situation.

The Power to Discern also calls the Shakti to acknowledge that logic alone is not enough. It signals that She must learn to hone and trust her intuitive powers, to allow the 'knowingness' beyond rational logic to speak its truth.

While this power is the domain of the intellect, it is the balanced intellect, the divine intellect. That means listening and seeing with both the intellect of the head and the intellect of the heart. If one or other is missing, then there is not the full picture and there will either be damage or loss.

Trust is a key word here and the more there is trust in the self, the more you listen to your own innate knowing that is born of your eternal wisdom, the more that you see the results in your outer world flowing beautifully.

THE ARCHETYPE
Shakti/Goddess Gayatri

Gayatri is Goddess of the intellect. She carries the discus and the conch shell.

The discus carried by Gayatri is often referred to as the Discus of Self Realisation, implying that when the Shakti spins the cycle of time, moving through the Four Faces of Eternal, Traditional, Modern, Shakti and back to Eternal, she clearly Discerns what is real, what is illusion and what is the truth of each moment.

The conch symbolises the power of wise expression, using the right words at the right time. Gayatri, like the other Shaktis, is bestowing blessings with her right hand. She is always found in between two swans, symbolizing the purity of her intellect, the capacity to use her 'seeing' to take only the pearls and not to dive into the murky waters of criticism.

THE DISTORTION

When worn by the survival faces, the Power to Discern is used to criticize and judge. The Traditional Face uses it to denounce beliefs, people outside of the safe zone of tradition in order to feel righteous and secure. The Modern Face uses it to argue, debate, denounce ideas, with a tendency to over-analyse everything for fear of being trapped again in false beliefs of another tradition.

THE VIRTUES

Clarity
Simplicity
Accuracy
Trust

THE COLOUR - Citrus Green

The Power to Decide

THE REFLECTION

Choice. Commitment. When I know the right course to take, it is as if there is no choice. I must take it. I have to act on my knowing, trust myself... back myself. Sometimes I have no idea where my decision will take me.

But just as the compass must always point true north, so too I must follow my true course with determination, conviction... and humility. And in taking this course, I gather new wisdom and I am changed.

THE STORY

I remember a great quote from Goethe that I first heard when I was doing my first self-development programs years ago. It was on 'commitment' – which I have to admit is an area that I have had to dedicate a significant amount of attention to in my life. There's something about the finality of commitment that has made me feel trapped, hemmed in, limited. But that resistance takes a lot of energy in itself, and what's more, the underlying thoughts of 'yes' and 'no' each struggling for supremacy, waste energy, sabotage success, cause self doubt and over time, create hopelessness.

As I went searching the web for the full quote by Goethe, I found a story that may be folklore, but the part of me that has experienced the power of commitment, tells me it is true.

"Until one is committed there is hesitancy, the chance to draw back, always ineffectiveness. Concerning all acts of initiative and creation there is one elementary truth, the ignorance of which kills countless ideas and splendid plans. The moment one definitely commits oneself, all sorts of things begin to happen that would never otherwise have occurred. A whole stream of events issue from the committed decision, raising in one's favor all matter of incidents, meetings and material assistance, which no man could have dreamed would come his way.

Whatever you can do, or dream you can, begin. Boldness has genius, power and magic in it. Begin it now..."

As I have experimented over the years with this energy, I understand that Goethe's famous words are completely accurate:

This is the story I stumbled across on the internet.

A small congregation in the foothills of the Great Smokies built a new sanctuary on a piece of land that had been willed to them by a church member. Ten days before the new church was set to open, the local building inspector informed the pastor that the parking lot was inadequate for the size of the building. Until the church doubled the size of the parking lot, they would not be able to use the new sanctuary. Unfortunately, the church had used every inch of their land except for the mountain against which it had been built. In order to build more parking spaces, they would have to move the mountain out of the back yard.

Undaunted, the pastor announced the next Sunday morning that he would meet that evening with all members who had "mountain moving faith". They would hold a prayer session asking God to remove the mountain from the back yard and to somehow provide enough money to have it paved and painted before the scheduled opening dedication service the following week.

At the appointed time, 24 of the congregation's 300 members assembled for prayer. They prayed for nearly three hours. At ten o'clock the pastor said the final "Amen". "We'll open next Sunday as scheduled," he assured everyone. "God has never let us down before, and I believe He will be faithful this time too."

The next morning as he was working in his study there came a loud knock at his door. When he called "Come in," a rough looking construction foreman appeared, removing his hard hat as he entered. "Excuse me, Reverend. I'm from Acme Construction Company over in the next county. We're building a huge shopping mall. We need some fill dirt. Would you be willing to sell us a chunk of that mountain behind the church? We'll pay you for the dirt we remove and pave all the exposed area free of charge, if we can have it right away. We can't do anything else until we get the dirt in and allow it to settle properly."

I had had my operation in Chile and was well underway in my recovery. I had maybe two and a half weeks left of my one month post-operative recuperation before I set on my way to Italy and then on to India. Angelica, my new friend who had taken so much care of me, had this sense that I had to meet a Chinese doctor she had heard about. One day we drove to his consulting rooms to find he had moved, as it turned out, he was now a mere ten minutes walk from where I was living. Just as we were about to ring the bell, he opened the door himself and ushered us past the receptionist and into his room with it is high ceiling, masculine mahogany desk and medicinal smell.

There we were, Kin speaking in his bad Spanish, Angelica translating in her bad English (at that time anyway) and me not really understanding anything. However, I was having the most extraordinary experiences.

As they talked across the desk from each other, I sat watching and feeling an exquisite energy opening my heart. I felt the presence of the qualities of joy and compassion. Later in the conversation I came to know that Kin had been a Buddhist monk for 24 years and for me this explained my feelings, as Buddhism is renowned really for dedication to both joy and compassion.

I sat there, my heart opening, tears welling and feeling very emotional. Occasionally Kin would turn to me and say, "Your only problem is you have to enjoy!"

Kin said that I needed to recover not just from the operation, but also from life, from too much work. I have to say that I didn't need to travel to the other side of the world and consult a Spanish speaking Chinese doctor to know that! However the lovely Kin offered me great hope. He said he could help me. But I would need to stay for four months without leaving Chile. He even offered to work with me at no charge because I was a 'religious' person.

My plans were to leave Chile in three to four weeks, but here I was being presented with a gift, an answer to my very own visualizing for the past year or more. I wanted to recover my vital energy, my life force and there was someone who understood, diagnosed, and was certain that he could help.

I had to Decide what to do. Abandon my travel plans, eventually returning to Australia, my family, friends, my cat and car, or stay in Chile. Kin had said that he would work with me whenever I Decided to do it, that if I came back next year it would be the same for him. But I knew that this was a gift of that moment, that there was some magic hidden within it.

My flight was getting closer and closer and so the next day I made the decision. I stayed. Then I made a commitment to come back and stay until the end of the 2006. And in the wake of these commitments, magic kept happening… this book being part of that magic.

There are many other external things that are taking place that are also totally aligned to my soul destiny. The chance to be of service to others, to write, to do professional work that pays well enough to work just a few hours each week, still travel to different countries, connecting with great people. But even more importantly for me, a place where I am able to focus on the deeply crucial work of the soul.

Here I am able to undo my old workaholic patterns. Here I am in an environment that supports me in remembering how beautiful and important is the power of silence. Here I am face to face with underlying old survival patterns that have emerged with great force and allow me to make some high level choices to clean out old power and control dependencies. Here I get to know the sweetness of my true nature in a country where the people have this quality naturally. Here I am learning to trust more, to love peace-filled living, to be. Here is where I am finding a new relationship with myself, with God, with the wonder of life.

This is what I think living is. To be tuned in to each moment, Discerning the special nuance of the time, and then use the Power to Decide to totally align to that time and commit to the track that appears.

In the wheel of powers, Decide is opposite the Power to Let Go and this has been my experience. I have to Let Go of fixed ideas, of plans, of old identities, of ego reactions, of fears and doubts and keep allowing the renewal process of life to cleanse and create each moment. And when I do, I am able to do the aligning and make the decision, committing totally with full power.

THE WISDOM

This is the power of truth, the power to choose truth, to stand alone in that truth no matter what. It is intrinsically connected to the Power to Discern, and takes much of its strength from that power. If the Power to Discern has been exercised well, then the Power to Decide flows more easily.

The Power to Decide is also associated with the intellect, but unlike the Power to Discern being an introverted process, the Power to Decide manifests outwardly. The one who uses this power is making a statement that "I trust myself and am clear that my actions are right and will bring success. I am prepared to stand by my choices and to allow and be accountable for the consequences. I will stand alone if necessary. I believe I am acting correctly."

This power is essential for leaders today. When most of the world can only see what has been, to make a stand, act decisively and move forward when sometimes you are the only one who can see, requires extraordinary inner power.

From time to time, it is necessary to introspect again and access the Power to Discern to ensure that the chosen course is still the right course.

THE ARCHETYPE
Goddess / Shakti Saraswati

Saraswati is also associated with the intellect, but unlike Gayatri whose power is an introverted process, the Power to Decide manifests outwardly. A 'knowing' acted upon has impact in the world. This is symbolised by the sitar. Saraswati follows no pre-ordained score, she plays out her own decisions, her own combination of notes so that the unique melodies resonate throughout the world.

She also carries with her the holy scripture and the rosary. The scripture tells us that her decisions are aligned to her truth and the highest honour, and the rosary that while she Decides for herself, she is aware that she is connected to many others.

The one who uses this power is making a statement that *"I*

trust myself and am clear that my actions are right and will bring success. I am prepared to stand by my choices and to accept the consequences. I will stand alone if necessary. I believe I am acting correctly."

THE DISTORTION

Strong Decision making doesn't need to come from Shakti. The difference, though, is enormous. You can be a powerful decision master, manifesting result after result, but doing it without discretion or discernment. If you use force, if you damage others, transgress your values or the values of other people in the process, if you make decisions based on your survival neediness for recognition, approval, power, freedom, security... no matter how powerful you are at manifesting, the results will never be fully satisfying in sustaining your needs.

It is possible through single-mindedness and determination to make anything happen. Mussolini, Stalin and Hitler showed us this.

THE VIRTUES

Balance
Wisdom
Surrender
Faith

THE COLOUR - Yellow Gold

The Power to Face

THE REFLECTION

I understand that challenges will come my way… that they come to test my resolve. Somehow it is not the external challenges that catch me out. The ones that would really undermine me are my own weaknesses.

These ones are dangerous to me… they would rob me of my dreams. They would cloud my sense of self and cause damage to my soul.

To these I invoke the fire of courage, and transform them in the flames of truth. I surge forth, boldly holding my ground, cutting a path of truth through the waves of the journey of tumult.

THE STORY

by Mariette Buckle

Who am I? I need to say goodbye to how I thought my life should look.

I am finding it difficult to face life, now that my son has died. I wanted to die the moment Dylan's father came, with a young policeman in tow, to tell me that the body of my son had been found.

I screamed and wailed. It was horrible, nightmare stuff. I was wretched. I pounded the floor, demanding it swallow me, crush the life out of me, so that I might join him, my beloved son.

Dylan had phoned me six days earlier, at 7:20am Sunday, asking to be picked up from Flinders St train station, after night-clubbing. I drove the 25kms straight into heart of the city. The mobile on my front seat rang – it was Dylan. "Where are you?' he asked. "I've arrived at Flinders St station. I'll see you in one minute."

He never came. I left a note on the car door for him, just in case, and I began to search city streets: rubbish skips, alleys, all-night cafes. I imagined that he may have been under the influence of alcohol and fallen down stairs, or onto a footpath.

It was so hot, Australian summer, and the Sunday morning city was coming alive, steaming with heat and people and noise and smells and in the midst of all this, I was terrified. Where was he?

I went home. I cried to my daughter, Alison. She was 18 and her brother, 22. My energy was draining. Alison called my sister, Kate and her husband, Michael. They came and gave me something to calm me down, help me settle while they phoned hospitals, then Dylan's father, my former husband, and finally, the police.

The week was a blur of phone calls, visitors, relatives arriving, police interviews, media, all seeking a young man who had vanished so mysteriously.'

Dylan's relationship with his mother was close. Although his parents had separated when he was 8 years old, his father remained a constant visitor. He knew he was dearly loved.

Dylan was a bright boy, an excellent student. He had traveled to London and Denmark, where he learned to speak the language and love the people. He was very social, very popular, and the media attention, calling for a missing young man, brought a flood of letters, cards and the question, Where is he?

'So when they told me my son's body had been found, I wanted to die. "How did he die?" I finally asked, in short, shallow breaths. Phil could not look at me, he answered from behind my convulsing body, still on the floor, "Suicide. He jumped from a tall building and landed on the roof of another." He'd been there for a week.

I would no longer be the same. My life had been changed forever and I could barely breathe. My face, the one which wore the mask of 'mother', was lost in sorrow and deep grief.

Five months later, in July 1997, my daughter gave me a brochure to the Brahma Kumaris Retreat Centre in Baxter. I went to be alone and begin my search for meaning.   already had a sense of God, influenced by a Catholic background, but I had not been to Mass for 20 years. I was 43 years old.

At the retreat I wrote in my journal, *"I realize how precious my own inner world really is. I keep asking for the realization of God, which is external, but as I get to know me, I begin to see that God is within me."* I learnt Raj Yoga meditation. I asked the questions, Who am I? and Who is God? Over the next few years, I attended many weekend retreats.

As I become more aware I am able to accept change without controlling it. This makes me an observer and I connect to higher ground. I recognise my soul being. I am not my feelings and not my body.

The path to higher ground is littered with obstacles and at times, I feel that I am seduced by the external world.

In early November 2003, I attended the first weekend of the Fifth face of Woman. This was to be an extraordinary experience for me.

On the Saturday evening, we were invited to make bracelets from colored beads, each color representing one of the 8 Powers. We worked at tables of nine, in the dining room, each one threading her chosen bead, one woman tying the string to make the bracelet. I had chosen the red bead, the Power to Face. I threaded many, many red beads that night, enjoying the smiles, the silence, the occasional word, and the warmth of other women.

During the final session on Sunday, before lunch, our facilitator, Caroline Ward directed us to our final task, a symbolic representation of the fifth face: Shiv Shakti; becoming angels of God through the form of fire, demonstrating the changes which occur in a crucible.

We were to go outside and throw into a small fire, a piece of paper on which was written what we wanted to change, to die to, in order to set about a resurrection. I wanted to experience this very much; I wanted to surrender to God.

Caroline put on some music to accompany us while we performed this task. It was called *Deep Peace* by Deep Forest, a collection of world music. It made me cry instantly, uncontrollably. It was one of Dylan's favorite CDs and I had bought it for him the Christmas before his death and had not heard it since.

My heart was breaking. I missed him so much. I took my paper outside, my tears flowing, and placed it in the small fire, the crucible. I was dying to the deep pain of my grief and the secrecy of this pain.

THE WISDOM

The main attributes of this power are courage and honesty. For the Shatki, the Power to Face means that nothing is too fearsome to handle, she is equipped with all the powers needed to face whatever comes, fears of overwhelming emotions, self doubt, family troubles, personal or professional attacks, obstacles, or situations that can seem impossible, insurmountable.

The Power to Face is the capacity to embrace even the most difficult situations, to know that you have the power to transform whatever presents itself. Practically, it means the Shakti knows that 'what's in the way, is the way'... that by the very act of nominating a different future, there will be a range of reactions that will emerge from others and from within your own psyche. Resistance, sabotage, anger, fear, anxiety and denial manifest in a variety of ways, in me and in others. Yet when these are faced and are resolved, the Shakti then has a way forward, clearing the path ahead.

It is not aggressive, but is certainly assertive and powerful. The Power to Face doesn't allow anything to hide, nothing dark or unsaid is enabled. This is the power to bring into the light of day the invisible stuff that threatens the new way.

THE ARCHETYPE
Shakti/Goddess Kali

For the Shakti, the Power to Face is represented by Kali because in bringing back the original innocence of the self and of the world, a lot of de-demonizing needs to occur. All the monsters of pretence and illusion, which cover the soul and keep it from God and from its eternal beauty, need to be destroyed.

The Power to Face is ruthless and does not in any way accommodate obstacles, whether they be internal or external. And she is completely fearless. The necklace of skulls that Kali wears about her neck, dare death to frighten her. Because she is fearless, she cannot and will not be deceived by illusion. She stands on truth as her foundation (God Shiva) and carries the Sword of Illusion, which symbolizes her use of knowledge and wisdom in her task.

This is the power to destroy all obstacles. No mercy is shown here and Kali carries the severed head of an opponent to show that no devil shall pass her by. In mythology, she drank the blood of the demon to stop him multiplying with each drop that fell to the earth. She will stop at nothing to rid herself and her world of evil.

She no longer accepts or allows herself to be made less because of her lack of value in our world. She stands strong and bold and yet is without ego, for she will not tolerate Ego anymore than any other destructive force. As she returns to her own innocence, her Power to Face carries the world with her. She will never accept illusion or falsehood, ego, greed, lust, attachment, jealousy or anger in herself and she will not support it in others. Her power is the Power to Face evil in its most overt, conniving and tempting forms and not be touched by it.

THE DISTORTION

When this power loses its purity, it is obvious that it becomes violent, destructive and damaging. Assertiveness becomes aggression, facing becomes ego-driven confrontation. This power then becomes a tool of survival, the warrior fighting for emotional, physical and psychological safety, using force to protect herself but not realizing the damage she causes to herself and others.

The added challenge that this damage brings is that it generates an onslaught of karmic return. Every action has an equal and opposite reaction. What you sow you reap. If someone is nasty it is hard to be kind and loving with them. Yes it is possible but if the survival strategy for safety is to protect and defend, it is unlikely that you will receive a natural outpouring of love.

So when you cause a war, you have to deal with the enemies that you create. The energy you send outwards, will come back to attack you. Then you will use the Power to Face again in the same distorted way, causing more karmic turmoil – and the cycle continues.

The Modern Face is particularly familiar with this distortion. In the Traditional Face, it is the energy of the tyrant, the dictator.

THE VIRTUES

Courage
Confidence
Determination
Purpose

THE COLOUR - Red

The Power to Cooperate

THE REFLECTION

I can't do everything alone. No one can. But when I'm clear and kind and acting with courage… somehow life works out. Opportunities appear. Synchronicity happens. And all I have to do… is my part.

Each one fulfills the perfect part in each moment, relinquishing ego and offering support and receiving support. And in the giving and receiving, life unfolds and destiny is fulfilled.

THE STORY

Tracey is a gorgeous woman. I only met her for that one weekend, but she left an impression upon me that stays today. She is bright and honest and courageous. Throughout the whole weekend retreat, she shared very openly and brought a joyful energy to the group. She was more extrovert than others, but in no way dominating. She was just plain lovely and fun.

At the end of the retreat, there was time for sharing. Not surprisingly she shared very openly and warmly, she said that she felt what she had experienced that weekend, was what she knew, she felt, she had been waiting for. She knew it was coming to her, had been awake and alert for when it showed up, and that weekend, she found it.

She asked me what the options were to continue to explore and study more deeply the spirituality and wisdom that had embraced her.

She was ready to respond to the signals, to cooperate with her destiny.

During the sharing, Tracey showed us all that she already embodied this Power to Cooperate. At one point, a dialogue opened up about partners, husbands, boyfriends, friends, who just 'didn't get it', the spiritual journey. One woman said she just had to leave her husband. I remember another being quite disturbed that this might be the future for her. Others started to debate it, while still others remained quiet, observing, in their own private thoughts. Then Tracey asked if she could share something.

She told how she was in her second marriage. Her first marriage ended when her husband, the father of her children, finally admitted that he was gay. While I don't know how it was for her at the time, she had come to accept (another Power) and be able to cooperate with her husband's choice. She didn't take it personally, she knew he loved her and she loved him, and both of them loved their children.

Then Tracey married again. As she began to explore her own spirituality more, she said she noticed that she was moving on from her second husband, leaving him behind. He didn't seem interested in what she was doing and she was no longer interested in the more mundane, meaningless things that occupied his attention.

I watched the women as she shared. I didn't know where she was going with this, but I saw the 'leave him' faction nodding, and the 'I don't want to leave him' faction, waiting with bated breath.

"I was thinking that I needed to move on and then I thought how unfair it was of me to judge him as so inept and unmoveable. I decided (another Power) I needed to give him the chance to choose. I sat with him one day and told him that my world has changed, that different things are important to me now, that I would love it if he wanted to be part of that because I loved him, but either way I couldn't turn back."

Tracey left her husband to mull things over.

"I have to admit, he surprised me. He came back and said yes, let's do it. We're still together, we're happy, we're moving along in a newly evolved relationship. Maybe you just have to give the men in your life the chance. Maybe if you do, they'll step up to the mark and surprise you too."

The room was silent. Truth was resonating. Tracey had really brought her Power to Cooperate into the room. She had invoked that energy or power with her husband and with all the women in the room who faced similar situations, and with all the men in their lives and the children born of their relationships.

It is a beautiful power that liberates, removes obstacles, brings hope and possibility and allows energy to flow.

THE WISDOM

In heading to a new destination, it is certain that cooperation will be needed. On the spiritual path as you evolve, become more powerful, less needy, then you are able to let go of self absorption which tends to be the current paradigm of humanity. And while the spiritual journey is utterly about Self, that is, self realization, self respect, self attainment, this focus on self is not selfish. Because, as each one of us becomes stronger in themselves, we are then more interested in being of service to others.

We become less defensive in life, more trusting, more giving and therefore more abundant. The outflow of energy attracts the return. This is the true nature of being - of being in relationship with life, others and nature. To naturally share positive energy through thoughts and feelings and actions as well as the material expressions of these such as money and useful facilities...and then to receive the return of these.

This is the power that means you can celebrate another's success as if it were my own. This is the power that understands that the energy of success is the ebb and flow of human contribution, of the subtle energies of pure thoughts and good wishes, as well as action.

This is the power that requires you to Cooperate with your intuition, your inner knowing.

This is the power that has you Cooperate with the omens and synchronicities of life, the signals that would move you in a more fruitful attitude or action to attain your dreams and to be of service.

Cooperation is the call of the time. We are all being called to share our gifts, the best of ourselves in the highest form to make a real shift in the consciousness of the world at the present time.

When we are in our power – that is our individual truth – we are aligned to our security and strength and can sense our purpose unfolding.

We are required to Cooperate with humanity, with God's divine task of transformation.

This is the ultimate task of the Shakti, the ultimate gift of herself... to withdraw from the pull of ego, to let go of how she thought it should be, to tolerate the challenges to her change, to accept her destiny, discern her path, decide how to move forward, face her inner doubts, fears and insecurities and keep cycling through these powers as each day she continues to Cooperate in the unseen plan of the Great Turning of Time.

THE ARCHETYPE
Shakti/Goddess Lax

Here the Goddess of wealth, Laxmi is the archetype for the Power to Cooperate. She symbolizes great beauty and harmony – unity. She is surrounded by many lotus flowers and these represent beauty but also purity and detachment. Her motive for Cooperating is always pure and she is not in anyway attached to the outcome of her contribution nor does she require ownership of the task at hand.

Her treasure of wealth is absolute abundance and is overflowing. Whatever she has, she is happy to share and in the sharing she doesn't dole out, but rather allows people to take from her store what they will.

Her prosperity comes from her ability to Cooperate and flow with the gifts of the universe.

The Shakti sets transformation in motion and the universe responds to her call, delivering signals in the form of coincidences and opportunities. Sometimes these opportunities are cloaked in the costume of loss, but abundance is born out of new space. When the old is cleared away, there is then room for the new.

THE DISTORTION

When in survival mode, without the wisdom of how to fulfill our own needs from within and from the Source, we seek to get them met through a range of different strategies including people pleasing.

Over-cooperation is a disease. Putting others needs before our own. Giving money to others when you don't have enough for yourself. Giving time to others when you are out of control in your own life's order. Always helping others in their projects when your projects fade into the distant past, unfulfilled. Letting people take from you what they want, leaving you empty and under-resourced.

When coming from Traditional Face, without regard for ourselves, we put others needs ahead of our own, subconsciously hoping we will get approval, love, belonging, security.

In the Modern Face, we can cooperate with others who seem on the rise in their pioneering rebellion against the system. This can be our ticket to freedom, but we don't realise that we will find ourselves trapped in their new tradition, their rules, their way. No change.

THE VIRTUES

Respect
Honesty
Harmony
Generosity

THE COLOUR - Orange

Final Thoughts for Part 1

The journey to empowerment is the conscious effort to 'wake up' and to stay awake and aware. It is the attention on understanding and learning that you and you alone can transform your life. You alone can undertake the road to recovery of the soul, the self, the 'I AM'. Along the way you will meet fellow travellers who can offer you insight, but the journey home to yourself is a singular journey.

Spiritual empowerment is distinct from personal development or personal empowerment. It requires one to practise the art and science of silence. It implies that there is another realm, a further dimension beyond the material where answers to our deepest questions may be found.

Spiritual empowerment is about understanding systems of energy, systems of power.

Spiritual empowerment is about learning the method of personal and social replenishment, rejuvenation and purification. It is about understanding the subtle and causal laws of our world, becoming intimate with the invisible things of life. It is a turning within to find the answers and connecting to the Source, accessing the power to sustain the journey, to clear the conditioning and to give courage to the quest.

If we wish to understand the way to our most beautiful and powerful selves, we must understand what will thwart us from our course. The habit of wrong identity, of believing 'I am my body'... will limit us immediately.

We will unconsciously buy into the many widely held beliefs about women that stop us, contain us, overwhelm us, belittle us, oppress us or force us to take on a modern identity that is supposed to be liberated but just binds us into other forms of constraint, limitation and often exhaustion.

If we are to return to the empowered self, and in the process contribute to others doing the same, then we must find for ourselves a new identity, an identity that is born of this time... the time of world transformation.

Shakti is such an identity. Can you believe yourself a Goddess, a being divine, an instrument of God? Why not? If you listen deeply within your own knowing and ask the question, "Am I here for a purpose?" – what is the answer?

As 'woman' you will flip between Traditional and Modern Faces because the qualities that we seek in each combine to make the total qualities of the soul... the full treasure of the Eternal Face. As 'woman' you stay stuck in an ailing system, beholden to those with the power to deign to dole out a morsel. Or you become exhausted fighting them for the portions you're able to gather in the form of laws, positions, salary. You may achieve equality in the policy and practices of life, but the question is then: does equality deliver contentment, peace and love? Do you then have personal power?

Having equality is a euphemism for being powerful, being independent, being in charge of one's life. But in reality, men don't have these either. So what are we becoming equal to when we seek equality? Will we ever be satisfied copying others?

As Shakti you will still create new laws, you can still attain positions of influence and be financially prosperous, but the difference is, you won't be bound to your creation.

You will have learned the method to regenerate the power within yourself. You will know how to create what truly makes you happy, to live your truth and to flow with the creative and divine force of your own being.

You will know how to forge an alliance with the only Being who has unlimited energy to share. In the process, you will have experienced that there is plenty to go around if the method is shared, and as such you will treat other women – and men too – without any fear or feeling of threat, sharing with them what you know. You will want them to be spiritually empowered also, and your life becomes a world of contribution and prosperity, of sharing and receiving.

As Shakti you have the practical powers to create a new path, to sustain yourself, to tolerate, to face whatever obstacles appear on the path, to be certain and decisive, to let go of old insecurities and to participate fully in life sharing your talents and specialities and learning from others.

It is a new model, not one that diminishes another as you become strong. Rather it is a way that enables all. It is a way of hope for our human world.

Final Step for Part 1

Because Shakti is the Way of Return to the Eternal Face, I suggest that you take the time to reread that chapter. This journey is not a linear one, rather it is cyclical in nature and as such The Eternal Face is both where we began and where we are heading.

It was placed as the first chapter of The Four Faces, to touch and awaken or strengthen that eternal truth within you, to give depth and hope for your passage. It would be good to reread those pages now, reacquainting yourself with the knowing, the wisdom and the feelings that bless you from this face. They will support you utterly on the return journey.

PART 2

HOW IT ALL SHOWS UP IN DAILY LIFE

YOU DIDN'T ANSWER WHY AM I HERE?
AND WHO IS GOD?

When my dear friend Mary Anne did a copy edit on this manuscript, she got to the end with lots of great feedback as well as the comment, "You didn't answer Why Am I Here? and Who is God?"

So here goes.

Why Am I Here?

The more you get to know yourself, the more you detach from the external identity constructs, the more you tune into why you are here. You come to know your unique speciality in life. Not a thing that you do, but rather all that you are, expresses into being, into doing. What you do from your essence is an expression of your gift to life.

When you experience the beauty of your essence you trust it more and more. The more that you come from that beauty, the more your life flows and you start to see why you are here. You don't have to think or construct it, your purpose – unique to you – unfolds and you are fulfilled.

A good way to check if you are on track is that:

- You will be very happy.
- What you do will be easy and natural and effortless.
- It will be of benefit to others.

As you move along in life, the doing may change but the energy or essence from which you come will be constant. Your unique speciality is something for which you don't have to study or work hard to attain. It is your beauty, your gift. But it requires trust and sometimes the courage to value something for which the world offers no value.

A friend of mine is a futurist and ten years ago he was telling people that 70 per cent of the jobs of the future haven't been invented yet. The world is changing so much. Ten years ago we didn't have the number of natural healers and therapists that we see today. Twenty years ago you had trouble finding natural food products. If you follow existing career paths, if you only look at what is already on offer, you may find that you don't live your purpose. Maybe you are here to bring something new, something 'next' to the world, not simply to repeat the past. On the other hand, maybe you will do something seemingly ordinary, not apparently new at all, but it will be the quality with which you do and be that will make the difference.

During a Four Faces retreat outside of Sydney, one participant met with our guest yogi, Dr Nirmala, for a private meeting. She was an optometrist. She wanted to change her profession and do something more meaningful, more spiritual, more purposeful. Dr Nirmala is a very pragmatic kind of person and she advised this woman to continue in her work, it was secure, constant and it paid well. She could then focus on her spiritual development without worry or concern about her financial wellbeing.

After the meeting the woman was not at all satisfied, and furthermore she had managed to lose her glasses during the meeting which had been held in the garden. She searched for them everywhere but couldn't find them. For the rest of Saturday and then Sunday morning she struggled, until someone miraculously discovered a missing pair of spectacles. Her sight was returned. She shared that she had been given such a gift. In the absence of her glasses, her sight was limited and she had felt unsure, tentative and outside the rest of the group. She had never realized the service, the gift that she had been offering all these years. She went back to her work with a different attitude, imbuing her work with a renewed sense of love and spirituality.

Content Free Vision
Most of us really just want to be happy, fulfilled, loving and loved, healthy, financially secure, authentic and peaceful (or

variations of these). However we rarely focus on developing the states of being, or understanding how to be in these states. We do, however, spend a lot of time, money and energy on things and situations and roles and identities that we think, or are conditioned to believe, will deliver these states.

The understanding of manifestation is not new. Many teachers talk about the power of our thoughts and feelings to bring whatever we want in our lives. This is true. But often we think that if we had a great career, together with a handsome guy who is rich and caring, and maybe some beautiful kids in a fantastic house, then we'd have a dream life. Maybe we would, but maybe not. That dream may suit your friend but maybe you are meant for a different life.

Perhaps you are a spiritual teacher, or an adventurer who finds herself in Africa saving endangered species. Maybe you're meant to be a mother to the world not just to two children. Maybe you're a writer, a painter, a dancer who will live in the south of India in community shaping a new world. Maybe you are not meant for a career, maybe you are meant to be a full time mother who cares into this world an emotionally and spiritually healthy child who will help to shape our future. Maybe you are a scientist who must use all her focus – intuitive and cognitive – to discover something for which humanity is waiting.

I have found it to be more accurate to trust in my greater unconscious knowing and the universal principle of abundance and right order, together with the divine plan, than to decide what 'I' want. I know that if I really put my mind to it, I can create anything. You can too. It is a simple formula. Decide, visualize, focus, take action, achieve. But do we actually, really know what will make us happy? I think not. If we did, we might already have created it.

What happens when you put all your dreaming, all your energy, all your attention into creating what you think will make you happy, and then it doesn't? You try again. Again it doesn't work. Again. Again. Then it is easy to lose hope. After hopelessness, depression is not far behind. So here are a couple of suggestions.

Decide to be Happy Now

Whatever your circumstances, whatever the situation you are in, decide to create as much internal happiness as you can, however you have to do that. If you know how to meditate, then meditate. If you know how but are not able to do it at this moment for whatever reason, then find another way to connect to happiness. Even if you remember a time in your past when you felt happy, then capture the feeling and intensify the feeling. Don't dwell on the past scene, just borrow the feeling. Tune into the feeling as often as you can.

What does it feel like to feel totally secure: financially, emotionally, psychologically, relationally?
Tune into this state. If you don't know, if you've never experienced these feelings, then imagine. Imagination is the wonder of the human race. Think of a story you've heard or read in the past where someone in the story embodies these characteristics. Immerse yourself in the feelings of that person. Borrow the feelings, then make them yours. How would you feel in your life if you were constantly secure? Strong and powerful and with all the resources that you need to live *your* life, *your* purpose?

Is being peaceful possible?

At our core, our very nature is peace. Practice the meditations in the Eternal Face chapter of this book. When you connect more and more to your energetic identity of soul, spirit, you stop being afraid, you stop worrying, you realize that you can't control things and you relax. When you relax, let go and flow, then there is peace and then miracles happen.

Bring the feelings into form

One thing I have found incredibly helpful is to take thoughts, feelings, ideas and dreams – which all exist in the subtle realm of the unmanifest, the invisible – and help them find their way into the physical form. I have done this in many different ways:

- By writing affirmations and putting them where I will see them regularly.
- By finding something that symbolises for me what I am dreaming into being.
- By making a collage with pictures and words that evoke the feelings of happiness, security, peace, love, security, when I look at it (using images that are symbolic only).
- By finding a piece of music that represents the feelings and playing it regularly, even during my meditation or visualization.

If I create a vision for my future that is full of the feelings, the states of being that I deeply yearn to experience, to be, then I don't really mind what the content is. My ego might mind, my mind might mind, thinking I 'should' be doing, being something different, something else, something more… but *I* will be content no matter the content, because my deepest needs will be fulfilled. And I will be living my purpose, generating positive energy in the world and touching everyone I meet with the power of peace and happiness and love.

So then, Who is God? and what does God have to do with why I am here?

The Word – 'God!'

The word 'God' has caused so much confusion over so many years. Horrendous decisions have been made in the name of God. Human beings have used the word, the concept, to terrify and control others, to dehumanise, to belittle and to demean. That One who is called as God has many names: Allah, Shiva, Jehovah, the Supreme Soul, the Source, the Divine, the Laundryman, the Boatman, the Mother, the Comforter of Hearts...

Part of the challenge in knowing this One is to go beyond the definitions and misuse of the name, the idea, the concept that has been distorted and maligned throughout time. For some, this is easy, for others very difficult. Some are caught in a belief that there is a God but that it is a fearing, punishing God.

The friend who prompted this chapter is an atheist. She believes that God is a human construct to make us feel safe. I suspect she is right in the way that we have interpreted, related to and understood God in the past.

At the finish of each of the Traditional, Modern and Shakti faces I address the relationship one has with God, the Divine, the Supreme, the Source. When we are in our Eternal Face, when we have returned to fullness, to our truth, we don't consciously have a relationship or think about or believe anything about God. We are connected with all life, we don't experience separation from anything, we are constantly in our own divinity, a mirror image of God and in that oneness. We are one with the One.

It is only when we become disconnected from ourselves that we start to look for Divinity again. When we identify with our bodies and lose the sense of ourselves as spirit, as energy, we enter duality. Body and soul. Polarities emerge: good and bad, right and wrong, happiness and sorrow, good and evil, you and me, us and them, inside and outside, and so on. When we separate, we lose oneness, wholeness, connectedness with all things. Then there is other.

When we split from ourself, we split from God, which is the spiritual umbilical that ensures we know we are always safe, we are immortal, eternal, divine, beautiful. When the spiritual umbilical is cut, we lose this knowing, we become insecure and lost from the essence of ourselves. In searching for ourselves, we also search for God. In searching for God, we are searching for ourselves.

Then are we also God?

Not in my experience. We are all definitely god-like, divine, exquisite beings of love and light when we are connected to our essence, our divinity, but we are not 'God'. In my meditations, I experience myself merged with the energy of the Source, the Supreme, I even experience myself to be 'as one' with that One, but I am distinct, I am I the one that I am.

Omnipresence is a popular concept. God is in everything and everyone. Sorry, I can't buy that. God in a cigarette butt or a fillet steak? God in a sweatshop exploiting children? God in a corrupt dictator?

God in me? I am God? Also popular concepts. Certainly when I am tuned to my eternal beauty and tapping my authentic power I feel god-like. But we humans are not consistent, we don't maintain the god-likeness 100 per cent of the time.

Maybe it depends on your definition of God. Maybe that is where the distinctions lay? I suspect that God is not easily articulated in any human language. As soon as we attempt to describe experience, to define the invisible, we limit, distort and diminish the vastness. We interpret the communication through our conditioned minds and our underlying fears and needs. So it will be difficult always to know for sure who God is, certainly through words. But we have to start somewhere in our discovery, our exploration. So I will have a go, presuming that I have enough experience of that One to at least begin the conversation if not finish it!

About God:

- Non-physical
- Non-gender
- Spirit
- Energy
- Never takes a human form or any other form
- Outside our human system of karma/action
- Resides in the dimension of being, of light from where we all originate
- The Ocean of all Virtues, all Powers,
- Always in a state of giving, never takes.
- Always full and all powerful
- Is not responsible for what happens in the lives of human beings – good or bad
- Is known as the Creator although is really the Re-Creator: restores us to our divinity by giving us knowledge of who we are and how to return to oneness, wholeness, self-rule
- Is available for everyone not through another person, guru or institution, but directly, in any relationship that anyone needs at any time. We just need to connect to our energetic essence and then tune in and connect.

Coloured by the Company we Keep

For me the relationship with the Source is first and foremost a very practical one. I remember years ago when I lived in Melbourne in Australia, I used to have a coffee every morning at a particular café. I would sit at the bench at the window looking out into the street watching the morning busyness of cars and people and general daily life. One morning as I sat sipping away, I noticed this little old dog, waddling past. It looked like a very old, yet contented short-haired terrier of some sort. It had a pointy face that looked a bit like it had got caught in the vacuum cleaner of life a few times. Its girth was thick, making its body round and just a little bit podgy. So that sunny Melbourne morning this little dog waddled past on its short legs.

Sipping my coffee, intuitively I knew what was next. Sure enough, from the corner of my eye, I glimpsed the other half: a man in his eighties. Thick of girth, with his neat trousers pulled up high, his belt somewhere between his waist and neck, balding, with a slightly sucked up face, short legs, waddling along in the morning sun, looking content.

In that moment I understood about God. The role of God, the ease of God, the reason for God. You end up like the ones you hang out with. People and their pets. Partners. Peers. If I long for my own truth, the reality of my own divinity, the royalty of true independence, then I need to be with, align to, spend time in the company of others who are that too. I have great friends, I am inspired by some extraordinary people, but none of them compare with the wholeness of God. And so being in relationship with God is a very pragmatic acivity.

Allowing myself to swim in the energy of such pure vibrations, such sublime frequencies – the language of energy – I am reminded of my authentic, original self. The more I align, the more often I remember, the more I connect to the reality of that being, the more I am able to hold that state in everyday life.

So the reason is practical. The experience just happens to be beautiful, sublime, exquisite. In that connection I realize the smallness of the things I get concerned about, the ideas I try to own, the people I attempt to control. In the wonder of that energy, I am totally secure and the ego dissolves, shrivelling from a lack of use or need.

The more that I dive into the heart of that Divine space, the more I elevate my own frequency to unconditional love and joy, detaching from the more dense frequencies of need and fear and shame. I become free to be me and to be of service in the world, in a way channelling these higher energies in places for people who are suffering, just as Saint Francis of Assisi inspired us to do all those years ago, asking God to make him a channel of His peace.

ABOUT MEN

This book is written primarily for women, as this is the playing field for me in this life. As I am not an expert on women, I am certainly not an expert on men. These pages are full of my experiments only, my curiosities, my wonderings. Having said that, I will now launch into what I wanted to say about men!

In our post-industrialised, patriarchal cultures, men have a raw deal too. While women have been on the road to liberation for over a century now, it is wise to observe that although it often looks as though men have all the power and the benefits, it is actually not true.

Men have been conditioned and acculturated into a whole range of experiences that are neither sustaining nor sustainable. They inherited the contract of breadwinner, protector, hero, never able to cry or show emotion. I recently read an account of the last night of the Titanic and found myself asking: why women and children first? Are men so indispensable? Perhaps it is as simple as survival of the species – let the children survive and grow up and the women look after them as they do? The same with war. Conditioning says men are supposed to be brave and women timid. Women have overcome this stigma to a large extent, but men are still burdened with the 'dutiful hero', 'success in the world' role. What happens when you just can't do it? If you can't bear the fear of failure or the reality of failure? What do you do? Deny, avoid, anaesthetize the feelings that are too painful to accept. What lies under the fear? Disconnectedness, grief, the sadness of the loss of a real life, their own individual soul life? But men have been acculturated not to be sad and depression is still a social taboo. Anger is easier.

I was with a friend once who told me he was going through the most angry time of his life. As it turned out, he was angry because he had spent an exquisite month over Christmas in a tropical island paradise, enjoying a beautiful, balanced life, which included doing a bit of work. Then he returned to bleak, cold, wet, grey work-filled England. And he was angry. I asked him which emotion he felt more comfortable feeling – anger or sadness. For a moment he looked a little stunned, then answered– "Anger of course!"

As women, is there still a part of us that expects men to be these heroic beings, even if we're now starting to say we also want them to be tender as well? Millennia of conditioning as women suggests a wanting and a need to be looked after, protected, adored, even if this exists at a subconscious level. Not for all women certainly, but it is a strong archetype in our collective consciousness. I remember when I realized that Michael was 'the one', I caught a thought that ran through my mind that said, "Finally, someone to look after me." I was rather shocked that I had such thoughts. I was a modern, independent almost thirty-year-old successful career woman at the time.

The journey back to wholeness is a challenge for all but perhaps even more so for men. The spiritual path is one that undoes you. There are times when the ego is dying that it is unbearable. The journey is a solo one, but it can be made more manageable to share learning with others along the way, to be comforted from time to time by others in the process. The nature of the modern male is that he is conditioned to be a lonely beast – lonely lions as one male friend calls them. So there they are, living in a straitjacket of a conditioned self, heading off to work most days, where they are not allowed to feel or fear, where they must succeed or pretend not to care if they don't, then come home to a woman who is maybe getting her act together and demanding that he be more 'emotionally available' to her. How I wonder? What does that mean to him? Where would he start? Life has taught him to compartmentalize his world in order to manage life in the post-industrial paradigm. And in the flick of a switch, we expect him to become an open, caring sharing kind of guy. But he still has to be a hero. And he can't cry too much or we'll start to worry about him.

And then we wonder why there is so much addiction and violence. Feelings suppressed with substances or action or work or sex or angry behavior. So many men project the anger outward rather than acknowledge inner powerlessness. I wonder how difficult it would be to be lost and alone in a concrete jungle, holding tight a volcano of emotion and the only one valid feeling is lust. Lust for power, lust for sex, lust for more achievement.

Of course there are men who walk a spiritual path. And they are remarkable for taking a stand and discovering their way forward, often alone.

But whether it is men who have to learn to be more communal, or women who need to be more contained, the spiritual journey is always one of moving to balance, to harmony, to alignment of our pure inner resources of complementary energies – the masculine and feminine energies within each of us.

And it is important to remember that we do our spiritual journeys differently, that we mustn't expect our partners, our brothers, our bosses, our friends of a different gender, to travel this path the same way that we do. We have to *be the change we want to see* as Ghandi put it. We have to use our best intuition and care to understand and support, as the men in our lives try to hike their way back from the wilderness to their own spirit. Tolerance, patience, humility and love. Maybe you don't want to do that anymore. Maybe you feel you need to be free from always looking out for them. Yet maybe, this is what the world is asking for right now.

A male friend of mine who facilitates spiritual retreats, told me after observing a Four Faces retreat, that he really felt that women move more quickly, more deeply and with greater absorption capacity in that environment than men. That maybe it was the work of the women to learn and change and share it with the men in their lives. Given that generally men don't 'do groups' in relation to their inner world, this might just be true. One of our colleagues in Chile is currently designing a new part for our Four Faces workshops on how women can best share this work with the men in their lives ... **in the way that men want it**...not in the way we think they should have it. Because we have to move along together. However, I feel that our part is to move to a new space, a new way of being, to hold a new vibration, so that it becomes attractive as an option. A place that is authentic, meaningful, whole, balanced and loving. If we can hold this space humbly and powerfully, then we have a future as a human race.

ENERGY IN RELATIONSHIP

Today I am reflecting about energy: energy maintenance and loss, and how relationships that are entangled even a little, are about energy exchange.

Last night I spoke with a friend who is caught inextricably in a political web of war. She is firmly fixed in the faith that she is right and that the ruling regime is absolutely wrong. She and her companions have created a faction, and it is undoubtedly 'us and them' territory. The Modern and Traditional Faces are fighting it out.

My friend believes truly that she is on the side of good, of truth. She is someone whose heart is very generous and kind and she hates to see others abused. She also understands the nature of projection and yet I'm not sure if she is able to see her own pain of abuse is what she's so hurt and angry about. This friend is a powerful character and would prefer to be angry rather than admit her own pain and vulnerability... which is understandable.

However, I'm noticing that being the saviour for her colleagues – although she would never admit it – is killing her gentle spirit. She believes she's saving them, on the side of right, and it is quite possible that all this is true. Yet in the mean time, her own peace and happiness are being violated. So here I am, asking questions like:

• How does one be active and responsible without losing your own energy?

• How can you be a confidante and loving friend for someone who has fallen into the illusion of heroism? For someone whose energy has become very negative and you find yourself drained after they've downloaded their story, effectively dumping their negative energy with you and taking your good energy? None of this is done consciously, but we all know how it can feel after leaving someone who has just told you how terrible things are. They leave feeling better and you leave feeling worse.

How do you protect your own energy?

From time to time, I still get lured into believing the illusion and losing my energy, compromising myself. However, even as I am caught in the old pattern, I recognise it these days.

Listening to the stories last night, I mostly just listened. I didn't try and give advice, well, not much anyway. I love my friend and naturally when you are outside of a situation you can see all kinds of 'better approaches' that you'd like to suggest out of concern, but mostly I listened.

After half an hour or so, I noticed how my energy system was feeling very depleted. I felt the edges of my aura were jagged. It felt as if there were a siphon inserted into my energy source and the vitality was draining out. I tried to change the conversation but it only took a couple of minutes to return to my friend's situation.

What to do? I love my friend, I want to be supportive, yet I've seen this story play out a number of times with her over the years. I realized I can still love her, yet I don't have to take on her heavy energy or the energy of the story.

Dr Nirmala is someone who has been a solid presence in my life. She is a spiritual traveller of 40 years on the path, and her guidance is always very clear and clean and practical. One thing that I have noticed with her is how she has learned to manage her energy. As a spiritual leader, she listens to innumerable stories of inner torment, challenges between individuals that happen in community, personal projection. As I reflect now, her listening is very careful. She is totally present to the person in front of her, yet she does not take on or take in to herself the energy or the story. I always notice that she sits as an instrument, not as an advisor. She connects to God and she herself 'steps aside'.

One of my survival patterns of the past has been the 'rescuer'. Women in particular do this very well. But it is a co-dependent pattern that is not really about rescuing, it is about making you feel 'good' for helping, while enabling someone else's victim status. Rescuers cannot maintain their energy levels. By the nature of the pattern of saving, you get entangled in the other stories. There is no 'stepping aside' with an enabler and before you know it, if you're not careful, a shadow has been cast on your world too.

Last night this is what happened to me. Subtle though it was, I got caught. I finished the long conversation and then I kept thinking about my friend. One thing is to be a concerned and loving friend, the other is to step into the darkness when really my job is to hold the light.

So, how do I hold the light and not seem aloof, superior, detached or uncaring? I could have employed Dr Nirmala's secret of listening as a clean instrument. It is not my job to save this friend, only self realization and divine healing can release the deep pain that is causing this intense reaction.

As is the way in relationships, one person is usually taking energy and the other is supplying. In this case, I was supplying but at my own expense. If I had been connected to God, listening with kindness but without 'interest' in the details, then I would have maintained my own wellbeing and would have ensured that the best possible energy was consciously contributed to the situation.

When this pure energy is contributed to the situation, then it disturbs the existing pattern, sometimes enough to allow light to be shed on the circumstance in a new way, a yet to be discovered way. Giving advice from a rescuing consciousness, is not allowing something higher, wiser, to emerge.

So today I am recovering from a Hero's Hangover. I feel the damage to my energy and even though I sat for meditation this morning, I was thinking about the situation and another quite similar one that I would have to encounter today.

I realized again the need for detachment if one is really to be a loving friend and be available for God's work.

LEADERSHIP

Years ago, when running a Four Faces retreat in Melbourne, Australia, I met a woman who had grown up in Bosnia, and married and began her family there during the ongoing civil war and 'ethnic cleansing', before emigrating to Australia. I asked her if she could describe living in the war zone. Naturally what she shared was horrific. At any time, walking in the street, doing shopping, having a coffee, there could be a bombing, gun fire, grenades. She had two small children, aged four and six. I asked her how the children could possibly cope with such horror.

She went silent, having gone to a deep place inside her, she said, "You know it is funny. When something terrible would happen, the first thing the kids would do, was look to me. If I was okay, then they were okay."

I think I heard this story ten years ago but today it is still as powerful as ever. In these times of profound change, of extreme turmoil, people will follow the ones they trust, the ones who love them and those with the most stability, constancy and strength in difficult situations.

Every other day I receive an email from some organization, group or learning institution trying to sell me a leadership development program. I have been someone who has delivered leadership development programs. Usually participants make lists of the qualities of great leaders, naming a few like Mandela, Gandhi and Martin Luther King (an obvious void around the women role models). People feel satisfied that they know and understand the competencies and capabilities required, they go away convinced that times are changing and new leadership styles are required, that Emotional Intelligence is more important than IQ, that we have to balance our feminine and masculine sides (although rarely articulated in those terms), that the new leadership is more facilitative and less about command and control. And they return to the workplace, with an intellectual appreciation – perhaps – but with no idea 'how' to do it, 'how' to be it. And very often no ongoing practice space to actually learn and become what they heard about and an industrial paradigm legacy of being with is the antithesis of today's quest for leading.

Women entered the ranks of leadership for real in the 1990s. Yes, there were some pioneers before that but they were few. In greater numbers it really happened in the last decade of the last millennium. Some of those women had the awareness and the strength and the courage to retain their innate knowing of the feminine. Some didn't. They adjusted and adopted the prevailing out of balance, extreme polar position of the masculine dominated way.

Those who held firm and brought their 'whole self' to work, using their innate powers to hold their very different way of being, started to change the system. Slowly but very surely.

One of my spiritual teachers, Sister Mohini, shared something profound for me.

One person cannot hope to change the system. However, each one can be authentic, true to themselves, contributing the best of who they are – their specialities, qualities and strengths. Then, the system will absorb that, and will adjust to accommodate the benefit. In this way each one can and does change the system.

After I heard this I was very inspired. I went back through time and looked at changes that had occurred within the systems I care about and have contributed to throughout my adult life by being me. WOW! I was astonished and completely encouraged. And in the process I didn't sell my soul. I didn't become a clone of the conformist parts of the systems, but managed to hold true to my own authenticity – at least as authentic as I knew how to be in those times.

So leadership, transformational leadership, can and does happen at all levels of the organization, the system. Whether that system is a family system, a social or community system, an enterprise system or a global system, one can influence, guide and lead.

While running a one-day program on the Fifth Face, one of the women shared that since having done the Four Faces her entire world had changed. She said that her family's lives had changed too. All for the better. She was so clear that she was a leader, that the new world of leadership wasn't about individuals leading masses, rather real leadership will be about anyone committing to being authentic and doing the inner work required. That real leadership will be about being an inspiration and guide at different times for each other. That the new leadership may be about providing leadership for one or two, but that there will be many, many leaders doing that.

One of my mentors whom I have mentioned before, Dadi Janki, turned 90 years old in 2006. She travels to over 50 countries every year, encouraging, inspiring and affirming this kind of leadership in the hundreds of thousands of people she addresses and meets personally.

When we were in Beijing together in 1995 at the fourth UN conference on women, I was leading a workshop on women and leadership and Dadi was a special guest together with a Senator from the Philippines. The Senator spoke for some time about the importance of university education and that in the Philippines women had this chance. And then Dadi spoke. She spoke for only five minutes. It was a powerful five minutes in which she shared that she had had only three years formal education from the age of eleven to fourteen. All her training for life, for the global role that she played, was spiritual education. Her soul, her character had been educated, that meditation had made her mind and intellect powerful, that spiritual study had given her the capacity to reason and decide and make knowledge into wisdom that transformed her life and the lives of others. That being a child of God, gave her the capacity to feel the needs of others, to under-stand the need of the moment and to commit to serving her worldwide human family.

Two days after this meeting, Dadi shared her thoughts at the UN assembly. She had been a Wisdom Keeper at the Rio Summit on the environment. She holds dialogue with some of the world's leaders in science, business, media, education and governance. She is not even five feet tall, yet at 90 years of age, she is a power-house of insight, clarity and experience. All with only three years formal education.

So when you go to workshops, seminars and trainings on leadership, if it doesn't go into how to become emotionally intel-ligent, if you don't engage in a process of life-long learning that is directly related to the development of your inner capacities, then I dare say you won't make it as the kind of leader needed for today and tomorrow.

As a leader, people need to trust you. When they are uncertain, insecure and afraid, are you worthy of their trust? Is your character strong enough not to compromise or abandon them when things get tricky? Do you know how you can stay in the light when doubt or fear would woo you to the shadows of deceit? Can you stay without compromise, in alignment to honour?

On this journey, if you stay committed to your own spiritual work, the strengthening of character and the illuminating of your soul, there is no doubt that you will find yourself leading individuals, groups and systems to a higher order of being and doing. Life will call you to that, in some form in some place, because you will be trusted as an instrument in this time of great change. Sometimes you will have no idea how to do what you are supposed to do – and sometimes even the *what* you are supposed to do will elude you. But you will know the art of stillness, the importance of listening and trusting your knowing, your intuition. And from that space you will know what to do, when to do it, and how it must be done will be made clear.

Leadership then is a service, a privilege and a contribution, not a position. It is a matter of Love, not a method of taking power.

MY LIFE AS A WORK OF ART

Today in my spiritual study there was the idea of doing everything in my life as if I were an artist creating art in every moment. I've heard that concept before, but today, it resonated in a different way with me. I went walking as if each step was an art form. I noticed that when I thought about other things, becoming disconnected from the process of making art, my body had strange reactions. A muscle 'pulled or tightened behind my knee. My hip started feeling 'crunchy'. But as soon as I returned to being present as the artist, my posture righted itself, I became one with the earth I walked upon and I felt the beauty of art in the making.

After my walk I went to the terrace overlooking the lush, tropical forest. There I practiced Pranayama – the ancient art of breathing. Prana – life force energy, or in Chinese traditions known as Qi. Breath, inspiration, life. Again I practiced art. Then to breakfast.

I found that in this consciousness I ate very differently. More gently, with a refined rhythm and a posture that enabled the food to be welcomed into an open form rather than pushing its way through bent canals and cavities.

And so the day continued. I forgot from time to time that I was an eternal artist making transitory art. But I looked after my thoughts, I clearly decided that I would not allow thoughts that are irrelevant, artless or without purpose to meander through my mind.

Tonight, my meditation was the most beautiful and precise meditation I have experienced in a long, long time. Artful silence. The art of concentration. The HeART connection with God. I had so much extra capacity to choose silence and connection without having to work at quietening my mind, that the yoga, the relationship, was deeply satisfying.

In times like these, I realise that nothing else but my own

divinity will ever do. These are the reinforcing moments of the art of transformation.

And so I will continue to play in the domain of the artist, sculpting each moment from a space of grace, unleashing the magic of colour boldly and beautifully into my day, looking after the canvas of my mind and heart, keeping them clean and clear and ready to receive a worthy work of art.

Imagine if we all lived as artists and our lives were the work of art. Stunning!

LABELS

One day in May in 2006, I was in Belo Horizonte in Brazil, where I was to go to a women's prison to do a two-hour session on the Four Faces.

As we drove there in the car, I felt a growing sense of uneasiness. In the past I think I would have suppressed the feeling, not wanting to acknowledge that I felt 'fear'. However, the lesson of 'What's in the way, is the way' has become so strong in my life thanks to my dear father Kevin, that once I acknowledged and accepted the feeling I was feeling, I was able to move into understanding.

A friend's favorite inspiration relating to fear is, "When you feel afraid, go deeper'. Inquire into the fear. As soon as you own something, as soon as you 'look at it straight in the eye', you become the observer, you become more detached, and it loses its power over you.

So there we were in unusually heavy traffic and what I was feeling was afraid to go into the company of women who were criminals, perhaps even murderers.

The *Power to Withdraw* was critical here. I was caught in some fantasy of my own making, of past insecurities, of projected beliefs based on no personal understanding or experience, perhaps more accurately, my lack of experience. And these thoughts were condemning these women.

In withdrawing from the fantasy, from the thoughts, I became the observer of the internal thought/feeling pattern that would have sabotaged our mission there.

Then I realised how lucky I was to have been given the gift of being able to think, to perceive, through a new set of filters. I started to think about how these women were souls, they weren't simply 'prisoners'. In the play of life, they were acting this role at the moment because of choices they had made due to certain circumstances or situations. However this wasn't who they were in their depth. My labelling of them would only create judgement, fear, separation, defensiveness, distance, mistrust, anger, and control.

So in those few minutes in the back of the car, while my companions chatted on in the front, oblivious to the inner film I was starring in, I recovered my sanity, and in so doing, I was able to return dignity to myself and to those souls I hadn't yet met.

We arrived at the prison. As we walked towards the double iron gates leading to the stairs that would take us into the large open space enclosed on all four sides by building, I still felt uncertain, yet more peaceful.

The women who were imprisoned there, were not aware of the workshop and now the guards went about the business of letting people know what was happening.

We were guided under the veranda, to a corner room. It was dark, concrete, and gathered all the noise from the chatting women sitting under cover on the veranda out of the heat. On the other side to the entrance, there were a couple of small high windows that didn't allow much light in but channeled the noise of delivery trucks. The chairs themselves seemed to belong to old prison chain gangs. They were joined in groups of three. Brown vinyl, tattered, functional. We attempted to make a circle.

Slowly some women started to come into the room. Their uniform was quite nice actually. Clean white T-shirts, strong, mid-blue track pants. Many were wearing knitted hats, pulled down low as if to hide their embarrassed souls.

By this time, the *Power to Let Go* had really been a good friend. I was having only pure thoughts, I had managed to finish any of the fear-based thinking. All I felt was love, and a strange and beautiful kind of clarity. The guard stood at the entrance to the room as a continual presence and reminder that nothing was private in this world.

The women were mostly young, some of them still had some brightness about them, not yet extracted by this cold place. Once they were all seated, we began, although there was a constant movement in and out.

I can't remember a lot of what I said, other than to encourage them not to believe in the labels that people would ascribe to them. I reminded them that 'prisoner' is temporary if they choose. It is the result of one or a series of poor choices for which this was a consequence. If they continued to see themselves as a 'prisoner' then the choices they would make in the future would be aligned to this vision of themselves. However if they could free themselves from that label, and if they looked after their inner world, they could start to make other choices.

I think this one piece of wisdom was helpful, but what I feel made the difference was that I had learned over the years, to *look* at these *souls* without labels. To see them in their original purity, before they were reshaped by our ailing world.

At one point, one of the women interrupted me and said... "You could be anywhere and you're here with us in prison! Why?"

In that space, in that moment, I listened and waited for the answer to arise within me.

Luck. "Luck." I said. "I feel really lucky, blessed. Here I am in an environment that is beautiful, rich, deep and most interestingly and importantly for me... REAL... no pretence."

Then someone said how incredible it was that someone cared about them. There were three of us there, all caring about these souls who had somehow taken a wrong turn in their lives.

After about an hour and a half, I suggested that we try some meditation. The noise increased right at that moment. Delivery trucks clanging doors and dropping goods, women's chatter echoing, bouncing around the concrete caverns outside. Then one of the women who had come there with me put some soft meditative music on. It was crazy. This gentle, soothing music just became another chaotic sound in the cacophony of noise. Off went the music! And we meditated.

I must admit to having no idea when I started, what the meditation would be, where it would lead. I just waited and trusted that I would be guided.

So there we were in the prison, me waiting, trusting that I would be inspired, I would know what to do. I have practiced this for many years. Angeles Arrien in the US used to begin her talks by saying,'My only gift is to turn up and see what happens'. For me it is similar. My primary aim in my life is to be available for the highest, most pure work. Sometimes I panic, don't trust and impose my own will, but most of the time these days I am able to wait, knowing that I will know the way, that it will be made clear for me.

And so as I began the meditation, I suggested that it was possible to find the silence even in the chaos of all the sound. That it was easy if you knew that there were 'tracks of silence' that ran through the highways of sound. You just had to allow your mind to navigate toward them.

"So as you sit here, either close your eyes or leave them open resting them on the – AHA! **There it was... My inspiration**... *the diamond shape in the middle of the floor. DIAMOND. Imagine a diamond, a beautiful diamond, but covered in dirt and dust. You know it is there, you can glimpse it, but it needs cleaning. Imagine that the most pure and brilliant light were like a gentle but powerful laser, cutting through the darkness that covers the diamond, cleansing it completely. And there it is... a pure, strong, bright, exquisite diamond. See it, or sense it, sparkling. Beautiful. Now imagine that you could transfer your awareness, your feeling, your sense of self into that diamond...Become the diamond...now. Feel yourself as this brilliant, beautiful, strong, bright diamond."*

And they did. The atmosphere in the room was so still, so silent. The trucks and the chatter were still there, but the tracks of silence were deep and profound.

After that they shared their experiences. Their faces were changed. Their spirits were changed. They had experienced the truth of their own souls and the power of that over the transient nature of the label of 'prisoner'. There was laughter and there were photos and finally blessings – little handmade cards with affirming words on each one, for each woman there. The joy in that dark, cold room was overwhelming, so much so, that it attracted the other women prisoners and guards who were in the quadrangle. They came and gathered outside, trying to push their way into the room to see what was happening.

What a blessing and a privilege to be able to share a simple yet profound learning, to be able to wait to hear what I should do next, to trust and allow and not impose my will, to find my sisters.

202 The Four Faces of Woman

STORMS

On the spiritual path, as I move more into my own self and let go of the ego constructs of the past, I will encounter resistance. The ego does not want to go, does not want to die. The resistance can range from mild to mighty. How is it possible trust that these times of torment, of tumult, are of benefit to me? How is it possible to trust as a general way of life?

Trust is something very, very deep, a great letting go and surrender that all will be fine, all will be good. It does come from a knowing, a remembering that all in my world stems from my inner stability, my eternal creativity. But for the old soul, the ancient traveler through time, this remembering is not always so easy. Trust can be a supremely challenging place to stay.

And yet, lack of trust is such a tentative state in which to live. Lack of trust is a state of fear, of tension, of bracing and resistance. It is a place of controlling. Of not having faith in oneself – faith that you can handle whatever comes. Of not having faith in your actions – even while knowing that good actions return only good results. Of not having faith in God – that by staying in the light your life is one filled with light and free from shadows.

I sense that dancing around the shadows has been a way of being, etched deeply within the psyche of many of us. Bringing the light of God and our own divinity into our worlds on a daily, moment by moment basis, requires attention. It requires commitment, it requires being present.

Conjoining with the shadows means avoiding feeling the fear associated with lack of trust. This avoidance shows up through a range of addictions including activity. Non-stop activity is a great way to not feel the fear of uncertainty and mistrust. This fear, indeed any fear, is a constructed reality, taking a component from the past and projecting it into the future, extrapolating to create a doom. And when doom is unacceptable or unbearable, you have to deny it, suppress it, avoid feeling it and so you do whatever helps achieve those results.

I've learned over the years to trust more. And that has led me to some remarkable places – within myself, in relationship, in meditation and in the world. The gifts of trust are ease and flow and wonder and magic. The challenges are to stay still enough, present enough, to recognise old patterns of projecting forward and creating fear through thoughts we are thinking. Fear is a belief that we have no power to influence the future situation. And that is simply a lack of knowledge, a forgetting.

You can continue to lament the past influences and choices, spinning them around in your mind, blaming others and life, or, you can realize that the past only influences you because you keep it alive in your thoughts. This requires great presence to recognise the many, many thoughts that swim around the mind clamouring for creative attention.

Every thought has the power to manifest.
Old thoughts, carved into the subconscious and conscious minds over lifetimes, have to be counteracted in a powerful and proactive way.

First we have to recognise that these thoughts are not real. These thoughts are simply residue, left over, like last month's Sunday lunch that has been hiding in the back of the refrigerator and is now rotten. You wouldn't even think of eating that, and yet we continually consume the rotten leftovers or our minds.

Our lives are created by our thoughts. If we are not choosing new and powerful and positive thoughts, we are surviving off the dwindling energy of ancient thoughts. These ancient thoughts may even be supportive thought patterns, but they belong to another time and place. They keep us locked in the past too. And even if your past was enjoyable and positive, it was the past and recreating it for the present or the future is dangerous. Times, people, places, energies and dynamics change. What worked yesterday, won't work so powerfully today and chances are it won't fit with tomorrow.

Trust. Trust that by looking after your thoughts in the moment, by aligning to right action, the future is assured. But also know that there will be residual accounts from past unconscious actions that have to be settled. This means that there will be storms. The ocean of emotion will rise up from time to time and in the tumult of the crashing waves of feelings, the magnetic pull of victim thinking will seek to make us forget our wings, to let go of the life raft of detachment and clear thinking.

These days I live in Santiago and I pray for storms. At least wind and rain. The pollution in that valley is so appalling that some nights when I lay down to sleep, my lungs scream at me with the pain of trying to work in this city. But after the rain, after the wind, the sky has cleared, the magnificent snow capped Andes are visible, the blue is so very, very blue and my lungs rejoice.

On a spiritual journey, there are lurking survival shadows, those past impressions on the soul that keep us from being free.

As we start to connect more to the light of our being, we unearth the shadows. As our personal axis tilts, the oceans of our subconscious start to heave and shift, sometimes bearing strongly against the coast of our conscious mind, causing us to doubt, to resist, to hide, to deny, to escape through some form of addictive behaviour – activity, food, alcohol, drugs, sex, or television.

If we could really trust that each storm appears to clear the pollution of the soul, that after it is over the lungs of our mind will inhale the lightness of liberation, we might welcome the storm.

I feel so happy to be here, so glad to have been offered this space. I am blessed on this sunny, warm day in June, having just weathered a storm of my own in the past week. I don't like the feeling of the storms, but definitely I welcome them, because they guide me, they point me in the direction of my deepest knowing.

The main thing is not to become the storm, not to believe the tumult is 'I', to remain the witness as well as the sailor. Crew the ship with all the experience you have, and use your wings to have a bird's eye view and see how you can navigate your way into the eye of the storm, into the calm. The calm is not the unearthed emotions, rather the calm is the eternal, gentle self, the depth. The depth that is recognised in God's vision as unique and beautiful, even if the storm sends you into disarray and you look and feel like a street urchin. Be cool. Remain the observer. Don't do damage. Clear the shadow, don't do action for which there will be more residue to clear in the future. Allow the past to cleanse. Stay present.

In knowing the way of the path of spiritual transformation, I remain wise, not easily surprised.

The storms make us strong if we are prepared to be powerful.

The storms make us wise if we are prepared to know truth.

The storms undo our ego if we are prepared to die to illusion.

The storms give us gifts we can share with others if we are generous enough to do so.

The storms offer us a way to move forward trusting life, if we are prepared to surrender to a greater understanding of life.

REFLECTIONS, PROVOCATIONS AND QUESTIONS ABOUT SEX

Passing by the local art house cinema one sunny Saturday afternoon, there was a young couple intertwined, immersed, kissing passionately. I watched, transfixed as they devoured each other. I felt like I was from another planet, just landed, seeing this action for the first time. Something 'flipped' me outside the system of human norms to be able to see with different eyes. Fascinated, I tried to tune into what the hunger was that was driving them. Pure pleasure? It was too hungry for that alone. Something else.

My own memories took me to a place of need for affection, connectedness, care, tenderness, love really, as well as feelings of vitality and power.

This was perhaps the first time I became aware of 'the sexual transaction' and the many layers of need that exist below the surface of physical desire. Since then, I have continued to wonder, explore, observe.

So what are the layers? Are they healthy, harmful, something in between or a bit of both?

Is sex different from sexuality, sensuality, seduction, sexual preference and choice?

Why is there very little conversation about sex in a way that is helpful without moralising?

If we could do a cost-benefit analysis of participating in the sexual transaction, what would the balance sheet look like? Would we consider our investment to be sound?

Sex has found its way into almost every part of our lives through television, movies, school, magazines, advertising, even religion. Something that is a very natural process of creation and propagation, has exponentially taken on tremendous significance beyond its function. Sex isn't really about the basic birds and bees of reproduction any longer. Its impact is more profound and at the same time is profoundly more complicated than its functional purpose.

Why are we so obsessed with sex and sexuality? What does it symbolise and offer?

And in the context of this book and the spiritual journey, how does this complex topic impact us?

In opening up this area for thoughtful reflection, I am not making any moral or religious judgements. I am interested to explore the questions. This is a critical conversation for me in the context of understanding how to master my personal energy field so that it is uncontaminated through dependency or neediness.

So these are by no means answers, they are observations that are inviting curious thought and personal investigation. Some of the things that follow are provocative, challenging and may not even apply to you. But whether or not you are ready to join me in this conversation for yourself, there is no doubt that as a race, we need to engage in some rigorous, non-defensive exploration about where we've come to in the sexual transaction and the impact it is having on individual self-respect, self-esteem, confidence and trust, as well as the effect on families, societies, the environment and economies.

Looking at:

Love, intimacy and connection
A body conscious society
The beauty myth
Sexual identity
Celibacy as a sexual choice
Spirituality and sexuality
Beliefs
Conscious empowered choice

A Few Observations

The following offers a very small amount of data that positions some of the impact of the current paradigm of sexuality in our world and in our lives.

In Chile it is estimated that over 50 per cent of all women suffer domestic abuse. Not all of that is sexual, some is emotional, some psychological, and for some women, they experience all three. Jill Shanti, an expert in domestic abuse in Australia, tells me that in most countries it's much higher than 50 per cent.

Church and other institutions around the world are finally looking at issues of paedophilia, where trusted authority figures have been having sex with children. While an estimated 80 per cent of abused boys never become perpetrators, 80 per cent of male perpetrators were abused as children.

In Africa today, the latest superstition around the cure for AIDS – a sexually transmitted epidemic – is that if an infected male has sex with a virgin he will be cured – and the younger the virgin, the quicker and more effective the cure. This means that men are having sex with baby girls sometimes no more than a few days old.

In times of war, somehow it is acceptable culture for soldiers to rape and torture women and girls captured from the enemy territory.

In many cultures, countries and religions, wives have no rights in relation to sex. The husband's choice is the rule. Rape within marriage is commonplace throughout the world.

Television series showcase different forms of rape and violence: SVU (Special Victims Unit) is prime time, award-winning entertainment.

Software programs have been designed to restrict employees accessing pornographic websites. Statistics in Australia indicated that a number of employees were spending 30 per cent of their working day looking at pornography.

Along with AA (Alcoholics Anonymous), NA (Narcotics), OA

(Overeaters), the other significant modern day addiction that is catered for is SA (Sex-Addicts).

Love, Intimacy and Connection

Love and intimacy are completely and utterly confused with sex. In a recent conversation with a very intelligent business professor, I was stunned to hear him define love as the passionate (read sexual) connection between young people.

So many of the poems that have been written, a vast majority of the stories that have been told, and so many of our actions, are in the eternal search for love.

Love. But what is it? Is it as the professor suggested, the hormonal lust of youth? Or as another professor added, the love of a mother for her children? Why do we search so intently for it and why is sex now assigned as proxy for love?

Love and Intimacy and Connection are impossible when there is fear, and fear, or versions of it, is always present when we are not aligned with our core selves. When aligned, Love, Intimacy and Connection are all independent states of being and are not dependent on anything external in order to exist – not another person, place, possession, or purpose. Once these states exist, they show up in all areas of life, influencing the relating that we do, the tasks we undertake, the places we create, the things that we utilise… basically, the way we live our lives.

When we are lost from our true selves, we are fragile, unstable and dependent on a constructed sense of self to survive – the ego identities of the Traditional and Modern Faces. These ego identities make us vulnerable and when we are vulnerable, there is fear, anxiety and nervousness, accompanied by protective and defensive behaviour. None of this is conducive to love. None of it invites intimacy. None of it enables connection. When there is fear, real trust cannot exist and so love, intimacy and connection are tenuous and conditional.

Under these circumstances, we can't experience the pure and

natural states of being that the soul longs to exist within. When we've forgotten that we *are* these states, that we *are* energy, when we no longer know how to *be them,* we go hunting outside of ourselves. When we've lost connection with the subtle truth of our own being, we then adopt the belief that we are our physical forms. Once we've succumbed to this illusion then it becomes normal to a substitute physical closeness for connection; emotional high for love; intercourse for intimacy. Through sex and a sexual identity we look for the warmth of love, the transparency of intimacy, the closeness of connection. And sometimes we get what we are looking for...for sometime. And sometimes we don't.

The spiritual journey provides more options on how to recover these natural states of Being. There exists a broader range of choices for those who feel that there are some unacceptable costs associated with searching for love in sexuality.

When you are able to hold these states through being them, then relationships change. No one is any longer threatening and so there is no need to compete for love, power or attention. The way that you interact even with strangers is from a space of love, intimacy and connection.

You can be an agent of transformation just through being. By being present in your state of love, you hold a resonant memory for others at a subconscious level and the truth of their own being has the possibility to then tune to that 'frequency'. In other words, you help them to reconnect to their own energy of love just by holding that atmosphere in your personal energy field.

The other thing that happens is that your eyes change. You no longer need to hide yourself, your shame, your doubts, your inadequacies, your judgements. You stop believing in the ego – where these all reside – and start to believe in the truth of your present being. (See practices in Eternal Face and Shakti.) When you are present in your truth, you've nothing to hide and you become transparent. Your eyes open to reveal the beauty of your soul. Intimacy. *In-to-me-see.* And this leads to connection. The illusion of isolation and separation dissolves immediately when you return to Being.

Then your world changes utterly. You move into life, into relationships, into work and play from love. As love. Then you have choice about what you do and don't do. Then you are free and empowered.

A Body Conscious Society

One of the big challenges with staying connected to Being is that we live in a body conscious world. Everything around us affirms our ego body-based identities. When we are conscious of our bodies and everything that goes with them, it's almost impossible to be conscious of our souls. This focus on the physical form can be dangerous, if we don't have …

The right colour body
The right shaped body
The right kind of face, eyes, nose, hair
The right brand of clothes, luggage, shoes
The right school
The right address
The right job
The right accent
The right everything else…

If we don't have all the right stuff, then according to 'body conscious' theory, then we ourselves are not quite right. But who decides what is 'right' anyway and have you ever noticed that 'right' changes through time depending on trends, product development and consumer advertising? So even if you're 'right' one day, it doesn't necessarily follow that you'll be 'right' the next. It takes a lot of time, money and energy to stay 'right' and each time you update 'you', you send another message to yourself that no matter how hard you tried, you're still not quite 'right'.

A friend in South Africa is divorced, now single with no children and manages to go out everyday looking absolutely 'right'. No one would ever guess that she herself never feels 'right'. She is at her happiest when she is cooking for others, taking the dog for a walk or having a coffee with the old man who owns the vegetarian restaurant on the other side of the park. But in the illusory world in which she lives and works, this simple happiness is not worth much. And so she constructs herself, her world according to rules of 'right '. But she takes sleeping pills, anti-anxiety pills, anti-depressants, is obsessive about order in her environment, spends a fortune on cosmetics and clothes, drinks too much, ignores or sedates all the pain in her body that is calling out to her to stop. She is hugely successful in her work but feels unworthy and unemployable and so is easily exploited by the multi-national financial institution she works for. In the end though, it doesn't matter what she does, how well she does it, how much money she is paid for doing it, how many accolades she gets for the success, it never satisfies the gaping hole, the emptiness and insecurity she feels within. In the past, this successful executive with the world at her feet, would take herself off to the office toilets, pull out a razor blade, lift her Prada skirt and cut her legs. It was how she experienced relief.

This sounds dramatic, but in this extract of one woman's story I see reflected many aspects of my own story and the stories of very many of the women I have met. The content and how we survive might look different, but the underlying sense of loss of self is the same.

The Beauty Myth
Pawns in the Sexual Game

How much money is spent each year on sexual identity and attraction power – products, programs, publications and advertising of these worldwide? Billions and billions of dollars. Maybe not quite as much as the US Defence budget, but much more than the world budget against poverty and hunger.

On a corporate assignment at a conference for a large fashion house, there was a public makeover by a make up artist from one of the big brands. A male photographer friend was working with me on the assignment. Together we watched the show, which took thirty minutes, as the woman highlighted the latest trends for the coming season. After it was all over, she revealed her artwork, exclaiming: "There... the new look for this season! Totally natural, you can't even tell she's wearing makeup at all."

What is the myth we have fallen for? So many women believe the hype. I know I did. The make up, the dying of the hair, the latest fashions. Even the anti-fashions of youth. For what?

In terms of resources, how much money, time and energy does each woman in the world spend on enhancing her attraction power, her sexual identity? How much competition exists between women at this level? In the end, is it really about the catch or just the chase? Either way, it's about energy, the unconscious expenditure of our valuable, precious energy. About believing that who we are, as we are, is not enough. That we have to look better, different, smaller, thinner, taller, more angular, more curved, in order to be okay.

A friend shared about a mutual acquaintance who died this year from breast cancer. This iconic woman was well known in New York social circles and from diagnosis to her death was just one month. Given today's medical research and capacity, breast cancer is mostly manageable if caught in time. However this woman had breast implants, and implants often mask the detection of lumps in the breast. Does it make sense to die for perkier, fuller breasts? It's a strange world when we start injecting our faces and bodies with bacteria and synthetic compounds, or surgically reshaping parts to 'iron out' the wrinkles and smooth the cellulite in order to feel powerful or to feel wanted. If we really understand that we are not our bodies, then perhaps it doesn't matter what we do with our bodies? It's just like appliqué on a jacket, or touching up the paint on the car? If we're conscious that we're not our bodies, then maybe. But the interesting thing is that most people who are conscious of who they are – the life force, the energy, the living being – seem to spend more of their resources on developing their character and then coming into the world of relationships on this basis. And this pure and powerful energy is their beauty. They shine from within.

Sexual Identity

Is this innate? Do we learn it? Is it natural? Watching a four-year-old girl perform an improvised dance full of sensuality and sexual nuance, one might think it's just how we're born. But alongside the four-year-old is her eight-year-old sister who doesn't seem to have any of that seductive energy coursing through her system.

Sexual identity can be active regardless of whether you have a partner or not, whether you have children or not, whether you are young, old, handsome, ugly, fat, thin, sexy or not. Living from a sexual identity is an 'on' switch, that is about scanning the environment at an often unconscious level and attracting energy towards yourself. Sexual identity is a tool by which to gain energy. It's not any longer about reproduction. Fundamentally, an activated sexual identity it is about being wanted (loved and secure) and powerful.

People use all kinds of versions of power to get what they want and to belong. You can even manipulate spiritual power and be attractive, a guru, worshipped. You can use psychic power – that is mental power to get what you want and get someone to want you. Very often when it's about attracting others, it's also mixed with sexual energy.

If you are in a relationship, it's important to ask if you are truly okay with the sexual transaction, or is it something you consent to in order to keep your partner?" If you're okay, then okay. If not, it's worth reviewing and assessing the value of giving your 'self' energy away.

In either context, you lose the clarity of yourself, the purity of your personal energy field, in the exchange, giving away your precious energy to someone else. In this kind of exchange, you may have managed to get some of the other person's energy as a trade-off which might do for a while, but longer term, it's not satisfying because it's not your energy – not you.

Physiologically, sexual intercourse can release endorphins into your system, sending you on a natural chemical high for a short time, but after the 'hit' how do you feel about having given away your power? Have you been awake to the impact on your sense of self – your confidence, your self-respect, your mood? Maybe the day after... or maybe a week or month or year later.

On the other hand, if a sexual identity or the sexual transaction are only beneficial for you, not impacting other areas of your inner and outer world, then maybe this chapter is not for you.

If you're not sure, you could consider that if you spend a lot of time thinking about how you look, about whether you are noticed or attractive to others, what you need to do to change the way you are to get a partner, dreaming about, reading or watching romance or erotica, being jealous or possessive with your partner or a variety of other compulsive behaviours, then you too are suffering from a belief that sex will give you what you want, which means you are likely underestimating yourself and are limiting your potential and possibilities.

Beliefs

Religion, sex and politics...universally thought to be banned topics of conversation. Somehow they conjure up from within, very defensive positions. Why can't we talk in a detached way about these things? Why do we assign our sense of self to our beliefs? Why do we hold a lawyer like grip on what we believe, prepared to mount the equivalent of a supreme court hearing at the slightest hint of opposition to our beliefs?

When I first heard the spiritual wisdom... "The truth doesn't need to be proved"... I realised that so many of our mental positions and defensive arguments come from a fragile ego.

Years ago in a pub in Sydney Australia, I tagged along with a friend who was going to her acting agency's Christmas party. At the party I met a writer. She was quite a small woman, vivid red hair, a bright and sparky personality. We started chatting. I asked her what she wrote about.

"My two favourite topics – sex and Chinese pop culture". Immediately I'm fascinated. "Tell me more?" I ask. And so she launches into an expose on highs and lows of her current sexual encounter. I'm not sure that Chinese pop culture was really of interest to her, because during the next half hour, she didn't mention it again!

Then she asked me what I'm passionate about.

"Purity – being able to find and rest in that pristine part of my soul," I said, and told her that I was celibate. "Oh my God, really? Tell me all about it?"

What I loved about this conversation was that two people with polar opposite experiences and choices, could engage with each other around the topic, listen to understand and not seek to convince the other.

Celibacy – A Valid Choice

When I chose celibacy it was part of the package associated with the spiritual journey that had attracted me, and my interest in sexuality in the early days simply wasn't there. So in a way, I didn't actively choose it as a singled out option in the beginning. I do think it strange that these days all sexual choices are valid – from monogamy, polygamy, homosexuality, bisexuality, multiple partners at once, self-stimulation and more. However celibacy is thought by many to be strange, bizarre, weird and even unnatural.

Over the years, I have come to appreciate the value of learning to understand and manage sexual energy. I think this learning is only possible through abstaining from actively using sexual energy, so that you can observe it, feel it, know it, recognize the motivation that sits underneath it...and then make informed choices. Our inability to recognize, understand and manage this energy in alignment with our values, has led to some terrible and tragic circumstances in our relationships, families and societies. Children's lives have been irreparably destroyed when adults have been unable to control their lust for them. Infidelities have caused wars to last for generations. What starts as simple flirting has broken up loving families.

After a dinner party I held years ago, the wife of a friend rang me and asked if we could have a coffee. She explained that at the dinner party she had realized that her fears were founded. She had believed for sometime that her husband was sexually interested in me. I didn't think so at all but I listened. She explained that in her spiritual path, she had spent six months living in community, learning to understand sexual energy. Her path promoted celibacy unless married. One of the things that they encouraged was that couples should share friends, not that the husband would have private female friends or the wife personal male friends. Until that dinner party, I had never met this woman, I had been a private friend of her husband and although nothing physical transpired between us, looking back there was definitely more than just innocent friendship. I felt grateful that this woman was conscious enough to have a mature conversation with me. Maybe she had some control issues going on with her husband, but from my side, it was very helpful.

It was at that point that I started to think more about the choice of celibacy and that it's not simply a matter of not having sex.

Celibacy is a conscious choice to relinquish a sexual identity for personal reasons aligned to your values and your aims in life. Traditionally athletes and university students would choose celibacy to focus all their personal energy resources on their field of endeavour. Religious people throughout the ages have found that celibacy can allow a more blissful union with God. Sex Addicts in the Twelve Steps program understand that abstinence is essential to conquer the out of control compulsion they experience. Even in other Twelve Steps programs like Alcoholics Anonymous suggest the importance of abstinence from relationship and sexual intercourse in the first period of recovery. Those on a spiritual path of self recovery and self mastery seek to control their senses to rediscover their intrinsic nature, their states of love, intimacy and connection, having greater access to the grace of the Divine once they manage to be in charge of the senses.

And while it's a choice, it's not as simple as turning off the 'switch'. Depending on your history, there will be patterns etched into the sub-conscious that are activated by sensory triggers like a movie, a book, a magazine, an attractive man or woman, an affectionate hug.

Learning to re-form, or transform any energy is part of the spiritual practice. But why? What's the point? Are we not just cutting ourselves off from a natural part of life? Quite possibly yes. Again it's about choices. And aims. It all depends on what each one of us wants from life. Sex, and a sexual identity, doesn't necessarily help us achieve our aims and in some cases, it may well sabotage our efforts.

What about Sacred Sex?

I was recently challenged with the idea that transcendence is possible through sacred sex, the practices found in the Tantric and Taoist traditions as well as the Gnostic practices. There is well documented support that these traditions do offer extraordinary experiences for couples, perhaps not all the time but certainly they elevate the sexual encounter.

However one of the prevailing challenges with holding onto this belief is that unless one is dedicated to the honest and conscious learning of the practices found within the traditions, it is highly unlikely that you would experience the kind of transcendence to which they refer.

The other aspect that is worth understanding is that the prevailing energy of sex in the world is not the transcendent kind. It is also important to remember that we are all connected energetically. When you go to a big shopping mall you can get caught in the frenzy of accumulated energy. When you leave the city and enjoy a day in the country, you experience the relief of being away from the energy of people and being in the energy of nature. When we think, act, be in the sexual domain, we connect with that vibration in the rest of the world and the prevailing vibrational frequency is not so elevated, so giving. Rather it is about getting, wanting, taking. The global sexual frequency is low. When you tune into the energy of sexuality it is difficult not to be pulled to those lower frequencies. Then when you swim in more dense vibrational energies, you align to other lower frequencies such as anger, sadness, shame, guilt, fear.

Getting Clear on What I Want – Really

This is a tricky bit, because what we think we want, is really what the survival ego wants, and what we really want are two utterly different things. We've been conditioned to believe that things, people and situations external to us will make us happy. We've been fed images of a fairytale existence that is absolutely unattainable and unsustainable given our lack of self-awareness and education in these matters. And when we believe, hope and fail, then try harder and fail again, eventually we give up in despair, sedating our sorrow with substances, work, action, excitement, people and things.

But if we can work out what we really want, and then work out how to get it, or more correctly 'be it', we then can recover our hope and enthusiasm, becoming strong and generous in life and relationships thereby creating a field of prosperity and growth from which to live our lives.

In the chapter on You Didn't Answer the Question Why Am I Here?, we cover the process of manifestation more fully, how to diagnose what it is you really want and how to bring it into your life as a reality.

In my case, I really want to realize my own truth, my own pure nature – the pure, authentic me – the 'being of I AM'. This is my aim. I have an understanding that most, if not all, the challenges that we face individually and collectively come from all of us having lost our sense of self and as such our security. When we are insecure we behave badly as an individual, a group or a nation. If we're insecure within ourselves, we feel threatened by anything or anyone that looks, sounds, moves, eats, walks, differently from us. When we're insecure, we see things through a filter of fear. We listen with distorted hearing. Our judgement is out.

So my aim is to go onthe journey back to complete security. Not confidence, but a depth of spiritual security that stems from an unshakeable experience of my own eternity. My starting point is that I am absolutely 'enough' as I AM… I just have to trust and learn how to be that more often. Then I don't need affirming and empowering through a sexual identity. Sex becomes a conscious choice not an unconscious compulsion to satisfy unfulfilled needs within me.

Conscious Empowered Choice

The spiritual journey is about returning to the clarity of your own personal energy field, beautiful, powerful, divine and unmixed with the energy – beliefs, fears or dreams – of others. It is about being solid in the identity of your eternal self, free from fear and threat, living in total security in the beauty of 'now'. This is the spiritual journey, the promise of bliss in each moment.

In effect it only takes a second to experience the bliss of non-attachment, of quiet senses that don't compel us to desire more. But it takes constant commitment to cultivating that space within ourselves, because the public world together with our beliefs keep company with our senses, luring us into the illusion of satisfaction to be gained from something or someone other.

Understanding Sexual Energy

Sex has often been described as sublime, exquisite, interesting, enjoyable, tender, loving, entertaining. Actively using sexual energy can feel exciting, tantalising, powerful and fun. But anyone who has been there knows that it can also be perfunctory, unsatisfying, demeaning, despairing, depressing, destructive. And once immersed in the energy of others, either through attracting energy to yourself or through the sexual transaction, you become bound in a karmic exchange – and an ongoing search to recover your lost energy, for you.

There is no right or wrong, no moral or religious judgement here, just an invitation to be aware of the impact that a sexual identity and the sexual transaction has on your emotional and spiritual wellbeing and on the relationships around you. If it's supportive to your evolution and undamaging to others, then go right ahead. Just stay awake, because if you lose consciousness, you lose everything precious. [3]

If however you notice that the results of your actions or choices aren't moving you toward the aim for your life, then perhaps it's time to reconsider your choices.

Experiment. Observe. Be Alert. Stay awake. The spiritual journey is a laboratory for personal experiments. There are no doubt some universal truths that support every human being on their journey no matter who they are or where they have come from. But even these universals have to be understood personally, individually, made real for each one through their own realisation.

SOMETHING ABOUT FEAR

If we are honest, a lot of our lives and the decisions that we make are governed by fear, in some form or another. Whether a mild nervousness, stress, anxiety, or sheer terror, fear is unfortunately ever-present in our lives. And it is not surprising to realize that it is not good for the body or the soul, or for any of our relationships with people, or our roles or responsibilities. Any kind of fear distorts our perspective, and we lose objectivity, clarity and the capacity to think intelligently. This is both a physiological and spiritual phenomenon.

I was about to go to bed the other night at the beach house where I am doing some writing. The lovely chocolate colored timber cottage with its cobalt blue window frames, is perched close to the edge of a cliff that abuts the Pacific Ocean. It was a windy night. The house creaks and the windows shake a little in the wind. They also vibrate every time a wave pounds the rocks just below. Growing up I had many recurring nightmares about tidal waves and tsunamis. I was haunted by the Pacific, as this was the ocean I knew growing up in Sydney on the east coast of Australia.

So there I was in Chile, alone. No phone, no Spanish, no car, in the middle of nowhere, just me and my thoughts and my feelings, in the dark. It had been a full moon just a few nights before but now there was cloud cover so I couldn't see very much, which made my sense of hearing profoundly keen. Every sound was amplified. My internal vision was working overtime. I could see white water tumbling over the top of the cliff, rolling viciously toward the terrace, clamouring its violent self towards the glass doors and pounding them down with a defiant crash. I admit to having spent much of my energy the past 36 hours on working out an escape route. Whether I'm in the bedroom, the living area or the kitchen when the big waves hit, whether it's at night or during the day... I would be ready. What to grab? My computer was the main thing. In this day and age, my computer has 'my life' stored in it!

So there I was thinking, visualizing, listening to the sharpest, most graphic sounds of the pounding, turbulent, terrifying element of water I had ever heard in my life. I didn't want to die. Not in a violent and petrified manner, anyway. I lay in bed, my computer beside me, the keys to leave via the back door on the computer, my shoes and a warm shawl all ready for a quick escape.

In my mind the water was vast, the waves were huge, every sound increasing the torment in my mind, reawakening the images from those dreams so long ago. Now I was physically shaking. Crash! Another wave. My heart was pounding. I was telling myself that everything was fine, that I was doing this to myself, that in the clouded moonlight I could see that the waves were breaking a good distance away and the noise was created by the rumbling white water against the rocks. I really tried to reason with myself. I had never had this experience of terror before where my body was completely uncontrollable. I thought then and there that if I didn't die that night – and I suspected that I wouldn't – then I would definitely leave this house tomorrow. No point in putting my nervous system through this every day for the next week.

I don't know how, but I think I fell asleep near midnight. The big muscles in my legs and backside were aching with the intensity of the adrenalin pumping through them, having been given the message by the brain to 'get ready to run'.

I awoke the next day to lovely day, the ocean calm – but still noisy – and the only clues to the terror of the night before, were the keys beside my bed.

Fear. Terror. Of course sometimes it is a very real warning. Other times, we create it ourselves, something in the external environment triggers a memory within. This may be something we recognize or something too subtle to detect – like a passing fragrance, or the feel of the breeze on your skin, a distant sound that normally is commonplace and inoffensive, but together with the angle of the sun on the rooftop... a memory is triggered. And if we are having something like 60,000 thoughts a day, and we don't notice more than maybe 200 of them, it is likely that we are generating fear-based thinking and feeling, unconsciously, a lot of the day.

When there is trauma in our past, sometimes as seemingly insignificant as being singled out in class for not doing our homework, or if we plant images and plots from thrillers or horror movies in our subconscious, or if we feel insecure, if we are attached to anything in a way that our sense of security comes from that attachment, then we are bound to be a victim to fear. It is a case of external stimuli triggering internal memories, generating thoughts and feelings to create an imagined Future Event As Real (FEAR).

This is different from intuition, which allows us to tap into subtle signals and sometimes even memories of the future. Some people have highly tuned intuition, which serves them well. However, when fear takes over, it consumes everything, including intuitive powers.

The physiological state generated by fear is what is known as the Stress Response. Under the Stress Response, the body goes into Fight or Flight mode which means that the muscles are pumped full of adrenalin to either do combat or run for your life; our breathing becomes shallow, our brain down shifts to the limbic system, the survival part of the brain. This means that you would be able to run barefoot away from the tidal wave, on the way gash your heel wide open and not even feel the pain.

I saw a remarkable story on the news one night. There was an American footballer whose kneecap was torn and half dangling down his leg, and with opponents chasing him; he ran nearly the full length of the football field to score a touchdown. Only afterwards did he realize that his knee was so badly damaged, and only then did he feel the pain.

So the Stress Response is useful for what it is designed to do... enable us to survive in hostile environments where our lives are under threat. However, many of us are living constantly in a survival state, feeling under threat, our decisions driven by varying degrees of fear, a fact that is highlighted by the fact that anti-anxiety medication is among the top three selling prescription drugs in the world.

In a session with one of my clients, she described how she left a meeting with her boss feeling really sick in her solar plexus. When she thought of the meeting, she still had the same feeling. I asked her what it was and she didn't know. Then I asked her a question that might have seemed strange, but she is used to me now and so she went along with me. "Where in your 'space' – that is, within your physical body and around your physical body – is the place of *clarity* for you?"

She thought, or rather felt, for a little while and then held her hands almost an arm's distance in front of her, opposite her chest. I then asked her to take the feeling from her solar plexus with her hands and put it in that place of clarity. She is a remarkable person. Although she now holds a very senior position in a leading financial institution, she is completely open to anything that might support her in becoming free from limiting beliefs, patterns and behaviours, and is always interested in learning new tools and strategies to enable her to be a truly great leader and make a difference in the world.

As she felt her place of clarity, she exclaimed out loud, "Oh my God! It's his fear." She saw very clearly that in that meeting where she had been very successful in driving a revolutionary new relationship with a traditional adversary, her boss had begun to feel threatened by her. The feeling that she absorbed in that room and was still able to tune into, was *his fear*.

After thinking about it, she decided that he didn't really need it back either, and then working with another strategy, she took

226 The Four Faces of Woman

the energy and 'released it' to a greater, healing universal energy. Now, all that may sound rather flaky, even to me. But it worked. Her boss is feeling more secure with her, and since then, he has moved to a position where he is recommending her as his replacement, which would make her one of the leaders in this organization of 30,000 people.

So fear needs to be faced, even embraced.
In 1999, I had what was diagnosed later as a series of mini-strokes. Using traditional Chinese medicine as treatment, my doctor worked with me on a spiritual level as well as using acupuncture and various other therapies to support the strengthening of my system. What we discovered was that every time I was confronted with conflict, I would recoil, withdraw my energy and close down. The fear I had of other people's anger, and no doubt my own too, was causing me to weaken my heart energy.

The doctor gave me some very simple and very potent advice. "Whenever you feel yourself shrinking against possible conflict, embrace the situation. Feel yourself opening up to the possibility merged in the situation."

I did it, and it worked. I stopped being afraid of anger or someone else's out of control emotions. I stopped being afraid of my own anger, much of which had been suppressed for many years.

Remember... When we put external circumstances and people as more powerful than we are, we are in a state of insecurity. When we put external circumstances and people as less powerful than we are, we are also in a state of insecurity. This is living from a model of dominance, which means that there is always the chance that one day someone or something will rise up and be more powerful than we are.

However, if we live in a state of our own truth, our own power, not referring or measuring that power in relation to others or situations, and wherever possible coming from a state of love, then it is easier to feel safe and secure.

And by embracing fear, it is possible to use it as a teacher to let go of and transform so old habits and patterns.

Back at the beach. In the days prior to the terror, I had stood on the terrace and called to the ocean, "Okay, come on, show me what you've got!" as a kind of bravado to prove to myself that I could face anything. I wasn't sure it would work, but I was willing to try, I was starting to be annoyed with myself at how much energy I was putting into concocting an escape plan.

As I yelled to the mass of water in front of me, I of course realized that this was a somewhat futile one-way conversation. Well, at one point I hoped it was, because really I didn't want to have to face a squall at all. But in this feigned bluff, I felt myself again in New York City.

My first visit to that place and it was just two weeks after September 11. As I arrived into JFK I expected the level of security that was there. But nothing prepared me for the scene on the drive to the place I was staying. Every single vehicle and almost every house or building, was sporting the United States star spangled banner. In the same way that I was defying the sea to do battle with me, the Americans were yelling to the terrorists to 'just try and see what will happen!'

A week later, after having been safely ensconced in a retreat centre in the Catskill mountains, I headed into Manhattan on my own by bus. Waiting at the bus stop, there was a newspaper dispenser and on the front page was the headline "Another Attack Expected Within Two Days".

What was I thinking, I had left all the people I knew and felt comfortable and safe with, and was heading into the heart of Manhattan to spend two days with strangers. And now there was to be another attack. The bus trip on the way in to Manhattan was about three hours long and was all a bit strange. The places we passed … there were flags everywhere. Vast ones covering tiny worker cottages. Small pin badges, adorning old ladies hats. Big stickers on suitcases, as if to say to any undercover terrorists, 'Beware... we are watching'. By the time I arrived at the Port Authority bus depot, I was a bit cautious. As I got out of the bus and began the effort of finding my way around Manhattan, I began to feel mounting fear. Again I felt it affecting my body profoundly. My nervous system was on full alert, my mind was speeding, my body and my aura were completely tense.

And then I realised. This wasn't my fear, this was the fear of over 200 million people, collectively feigning power but feeling utterly powerless. I was tapping into their national terror in the same way that my client had tapped into her boss's fear.

Once I realised that, I could have a strategy for managing myself during the next two days and beyond. While I was passive, I was like a sponge, absorbing the vibrations around and those vibrations were triggering connected and vaguely connected memories in my subconscious.

However, if I were to become active, then I would manage my own energy, not be a sponge and would be able to be of service, to help in a way that I knew I could. I would generate peace and spread that vibe around me as I moved through the city. And that's what I did. Even being outside the Rockerfeller Center on the day it was evacuated with the anthrax scare didn't shake me once I was anchored in this original state of Being.

This is a powerful strategy. Generate positive vibrations and donate them to those around you. In that way I was able to remain secure and calm – and so can anyone who tries this.

In Capetown, South Africa, in 1999, I was running a workshop on the Four Faces at the World Parliament of Religions. One of the women in the workshop shared a very challenging and inspiring story that has stayed with me all these years later.

She had been living in Mauritius for the many years of the South African struggle against Apartheid and had only returned sometime after Mandela was in office and the dreadful regime of outrageous discrimination had officially dissolved. She was living with her mother. However, as she described, it wasn't really living at all. Her mother was too fearful to leave the house – ever. She had barbed wire and broken glass atop the fences surrounding the entire house, alarm systems, dogs and security guards. All this was her mother's fear, but she felt trapped, stifled, a prisoner in her own home. And she had begun to be captured by the same terror as her mother. She said that she knew that if she was going to stay in Johannesburg, or even South Africa, then she would have to find a way to live without fear.

So one day, she packed a small backpack, and to manage her mother's fear, she told her she was going to visit friends for a while down south. What she had really decided to do rid herself of fear. She committed to herself that she would just walk and see what happened. She would take a ride with whoever offered her a ride. She would accept offers of accommodation from whoever offered. She would sleep in parks if that was all that was available. From memory she spent almost two months 'out'. She caught collective taxis that were for 'coloureds' or blacks. She accepted invitations to dine in the homes of people she didn't know. She slept in parks and in strange beds offered by kind strangers.

She told us that there were times that she did feel fear, but that the fear was born inside her, that there was nothing in her environment to be feared. If she consciously stayed 'in the light', there really was nothing to fear. And this was her gift to South Africa. "Small though it is," she said, "I can at least share that with my country. I'm only one person, but I live in the heart of Johannesburg, without even a drop of fear."

Shifting consciousness, recognizing the reality of being the light and not the shadows of doubt and fear, being able to detach from thoughts and feelings, is a critical step in being able to transform fear and powerlessness.

A friend went back to university to study film making when she was 40. One night in her second year, she had been at school in the editing suite until late. It was winter and as she waited in the dark, cold, deserted night, around 11pm, she became aware of that she was no longer alone. As she waited for the train to take her home to her nice warm bed, there was a gang of young men moving directly toward her.

She told me that she knew that any moment fear could grip her and she would be lost, powerless. Then she took hold of her thoughts and told herself that she hadn't been working with this spiritual stuff for 20 years to have it desert her now.

So she just shifted consciousness and became 'Shakti'. As she did this, without thinking, she knew exactly what to do. She turned in the direction of the young men and started walking purposely toward them. They answered by moving faster toward her. As they got closer, one of them yelled out "what the f*** are you lookin' at?" Without thinking about her response, but from a position of feeling powerful, she saw this guy in his T-shirt and responded immediately. "I'm lookin' at you and thinking you must be incredibly cold".

That was it. He stopped short. "Yeah some bastard stole my jacket on the train."

My friend's response, "What's the world coming to?"

"I know… it sucks!" And there they stood for the next ten minutes until her train arrived, talking about the state of the world, the inequities, the deterioration of the human spirit.

"Well guys, this is my train… it has been nice talking to you."

"Yeah…nice talkin' to you too. You take care now."

And off she went safely home to bed.

Not only did this friend manage to turn a fearful and potentially dangerous situation around by shifting her consciousness, her sense of self, she also gave those young guys a different experience from what they are used to, offering them an expanded view of the world.

At the beach again, back to the day after the terror of the night before... I decided bravado wouldn't do it. I needed a new strategy. Some friends dropped by with some supplies and assured me that although the house was *very close* to the edge of the cliff, they were certain I would be okay. If there was a tsunami someone would come for me... even in the dark. I had thought all this through before and it hadn't stopped me from going through the torture of the previous night.

Now this may sound ridiculous, but I realized that I had to love the ocean. I had to return to love. And I questioned that if I were to die - and we all do have to leave this body at some time - did I want to leave in a state of fear, of terror, or a state of love? In fear, I was obsessed by what threatened me. I wasn't able to think anything positive. I definitely wasn't able to remember God and draw on the beauty of that energy. In fear, I had abandoned myself and if I were to die, I would die alone and bereft. Not a nice way for the soul to complete one life and begin the next. Okay then, how did I want to live? In fear, terror or love? That was easy to answer. Love of course.

Out onto the terrace again and I changed the way I saw the ocean. I changed my state to my spiritual identity, the eternal being of light, and this changed my thoughts and the feelings I had about the ocean. In my mind's eye, I saw that the waves were a reasonable size, rather than the giants I had been manufacturing in my mind during the previous week. I became positively active in my relationship with the ocean, rather than being a passive receiver of sounds, feelings, images, all triggering past memories. In this active state of loving-ness, fear simply didn't exist.

Fear of Rejection

In fact, I had done the same thing years ago but in relation to people. I realized that I felt tentative, circumspect and even nervous when coming into relationship with certain people. This fear would cause me to be cautious and at times, inauthentic.

It was based on a real fear of rejection and so I created escape routes, telling myself that I didn't want to do this or that, or I didn't have time or interest, simply to avoid the possibility of rejection. I realized that this fear had accompanied me much of my life and I was really ready for it to finish.

I was in India on retreat at the time, and in my meditation I simply caught the clue 'love'.

Of course, the fear of rejection is based on wanting acceptance, giving someone else the power to accept you or not, approve you or not. But to go into a situation or relationship in a state of love, a state of emanating rather than wanting, completely changes the dynamic from powerless to powerful... from fearful to loving. In that way you have nothing to lose and you are secure enough to be your authentic self.

So loving the ocean, the days passed and I stopped thinking of escape routes. Yes I admit to standing on the terrace one day and closing my eyes to accustom myself the sound of the waves and the winds so that I wouldn't be deceived again by my senses in the dark. But I did this with love.

I stopped noticing the sound, it somehow became a soothing backdrop, and as the house rattled around me, I worked and slept easily and well.

THE LENSES THROUGH WHICH WE SEE

Accessing memories of the past isn't always easy. During a retreat in Brazil we made an exercise to think back through one's life and map the highlights – the high, bright moments as well as the low times. I spent quite a bit of time explaining this process. A fictitious example is below.

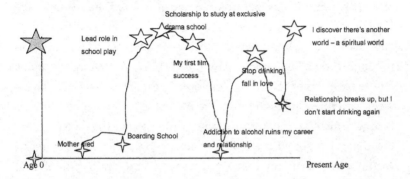

So after a long explanation, I set them all to work. I saw the look of complete disturbance on one woman's face. I asked if there were any more questions. This woman, Maria, said that it wasn't possible for her to find any bright spots, any high times, that her life had been only dark times.

I told Maria the story of how I had believed that my teenage years had been somewhat tragic, that I managed to 'gestalt' all experiences into one label and then believe that label to be true.

Around the year 2000 I had to do some work for a large bank. Somehow I mixed up the timing of the workshop and I didn't turn up to one of the sessions. People had travelled from all areas of Sydney to attend this focus group. I apologized and promised that I would travel to the different groups and that there would be no extra charge of course.

One of the groups was in the place where I had gone to school, where I had my first job, where I worked part-time while at school, where my first boyfriend worked as a jeweller, where I went to my first dance and many other dances right through to my early twenties. I had a 40-minute train trip out to the satellite city of Parramatta. I had travelled this route everyday for almost two years when I was 20, going to work in the city.

I was absolutely certain that as I travelled on that train through the suburbs heading west, I would feel all kinds of sad and dramatic feelings linking me to the 'tragedy' of my younger existence. But no. I just saw a lot of houses. I saw the station where I had lived with Karen Weston, who had been such an incredible support for me when I was exploring whether or not I wanted to pursue acting as a career. I saw the Auburn and Granville pools where my mother took me to go to swimming training five days a week when I was much younger. We passed under the Granville Bridge which had collapsed one morning when the 8.06am from Parramatta derailed and killed many people. On another day I would have been on that train. And as the train pulled into Parramatta, I thought that I would feel sick with feelings of the unhappiness of the past. But I didn't.

It was a bright sunny day, and the station was clean, and the people were going about their business. I was early and so I decided to take myself on a short tour around the city to continue the process of undoing my distorted memories. I went to the shopping centre where I had worked in the department store part-time while still at school. I saw the place where I had my first job after leaving school. I walked to where my boyfriend had worked as a jeweller with his father. He was no longer there, but somehow I found his new studio. And there he was, 20 years older but still looking and sounding the same. Still surfing. Finally I went to the bank and did my work. I went back to the train and headed back to Sydney, having experienced a new relationship with my past.

How we look at things determines our experience of those things. Two people can see the same scene and have two very different experiences. Perception is not always real and it is never absolute. It is shaped by our conditioning, our knowledge, our experience, and our present state of mine.

Victor Frankl tells his experience of the German concentration camp and how he observed that different people survived their time in the camps in different ways. He watched as people arrived and noticed that some were able to maintain their life force energy and dignity while others faded from life even before they were taken to the gas chamber.

When he analyzed the difference, he identified that there was a moment between the external stimulus and response. He concluded that this moment was where freedom, where power, where choice existed. You can control your response. Your thoughts, your response, your life – all are your own. Everything depends on how your orient your perception.

Back at the retreat, I sent the group to work on their map. Within about three minutes, Maria's face had completely changed. "I found some high times, some bright moments in my life!"

Memories are not real. Don't believe them. If there are memories that haunt you, chase you, keep you from flying, go back into the memories as an adult and choose new ones, wise ones, supportive ones.

Sometimes it is necessary to rewrite, reinterpret the stories of our lives, to use some method to help us undo the distortion or the imprinting that limits us today. There are a range of different methods available to do this work, and sometimes it is useful to seek professional help from a psychotherapist for some time. The challenge, of course, is to find the right one, to be sure that the person you work with values your process and is present to you, and determined that you remain independent from them.

Recovering Innocence and Self Respect

"That which you don't own will rise up and become hostile."

Anyone who is an 'old soul' will have things in their past which they are not happy about, things where they compromised their dignity or someone else's. A useful process is to write your remembered history as a detached observer. To understand that as spiritual beings who lost our sense of self and our spiritual resources, we behaved in ways that were aimed at fulfilling our lack. Whether we sought love, power, security, freedom or truth, without a strong sense of our own eternal worth, we will have done certain things that in retrospect we wish hadn't. However, these were the only choices we could make at that time given our resources.

It is helpful to remember that we have deep influences in the soul from past lives. Each one is an eternal traveller who has been losing 'pure self' energy throughout time. By referring externally for a sense of self, you automatically step away from your own core of strength, giving power to others to determine who you are. And they do the same with us. And we reshape each other into vague semblances of strange selves we've forgotten. And we are never satisfied... with ourselves or others.

Recently I met a remarkable women at a Four Faces retreat in Canela in the south of Brazil. She was around 75 years of age, an incredibly bright and positive woman. Later I learned her story. That afternoon, her husband Bill came and collected her. Bill was from the United States, and he was in his late eighties. They had been married for 37 years. This day was the first time they had been separated for longer than two hours in all that time. She told me that even during a two hour separation they would telephone each other ten times. However on first day apart in 37 years, she didn't call home even once.

For me, a chronic defender of personal space and independence in relationship, I couldn't imagine such a thing. They went on to tell me that in all their years of marriage, not once had they raised their voices to each other, not once had they argued. Coming from my family where there were lots of arguments and raised voices, this was unimaginable. "That's because I always say *yes*," chimed in the husband from the front seat of the warm and comfortable car. "So do I," she said.

This secret is very powerful. To always say yes to another that we're in equal relationship with, yes from the heart. Imagine never being blocked, always being enabled. What might that do for your confidence, your sense of self, and self worth.

The Brahma Kumaris World Spiritual University leadership group is a collection of women elders in their eighties and nineties. When they took the full and formal lead of the organization, they were in their fifties. One of the principles that they agreed to was 'One suggests, the others accept'. They knew that they had to remain unified and supportive and powerful together if they were to carry on their work of re-awakening spiritual awareness and peace in the hearts and minds of humanity.

It seems to me from the outside that they decided to trust each other, understanding that an activity or an action that was suggested could do no harm. There might be a better way to do something but their harmony and unity was not worth sacrificing for a slightly improved system or program. The energy of allowing, of trust, of unfolding of believing that 'the right thing will happen', that God's energy was most important anyway… all of this has meant that in the past 38 years, these women have provided leadership for millions people in over a hundred countries.

The energy of 'no' stops everything. It finishes love, it destroys trust, it annihilates confidence, it cripples commitment. Erika who used to work with me, would always say 'Caroline, the right thing will happen.'

In the scheme of things, I have to ask myself the question,

'How do I know what is the right thing anyway'. The world is much more vast than the capacity of my attached intellect. However, in the context of life and love and a journey that is about returning to the wonder of being, it is important to discern when it is critical to share a strong intuition and when it is just the ego's need to feel heard. Or maybe, having good wishes and strong faith in the 'right thing happening' is all that is needed.

This is not quite as easy as it sounds, of course. The survival faces of right and wrong, good and bad, judgement and approval, will seek to undermine this decision. The ego's righteous anger will want to justify the validity of reaction, of a lawyer-like attempt to turn the events in favour of truth or freedom or the right to free speech.

However with either face, no matter how right they may seem, they steal away innocence. They rob us of ourselves. They make us prisoner to the past and other people and old systems and fear and insecurity. They contaminate our lives while trying to protect them. Because these faces are ignorant, they live only because we forgot that at core, we are beauty and strength and clarity, with the ability to choose right action and even stand alone if we must.

These faces believe the memories. They don't understand that there is a greater plan, a miraculous cosmic undertaking that is happening around us, and that we are tiny and insignificant, yet paradoxically, important pieces of that plan. They are based in fear and insecurity and keep us separate from life and trust and love and God and the very truth of our own life force energy.

And so a simple practice of Shakti is to say 'yes'. If you notice that you are a 'blocker', a criticizer, someone whose idea is always better than the rest, this is a good practice.

Unblocking Valuable Energy
Firstly say 'yes' to your destiny. What might it be like to trust that you're not alone, that the hand of the Divine is with you always, guiding you easily if you can only listen.

Saying 'Yes' means you don't have to think too much.

'Yes' means that the energy of flow is present in your life.

'Yes' means that resistance disappears and this frees up an enormous amount of energy.

'Yes' to others means you stop trying to control the whole world.

'Yes, show me how," makes you humble, and humility allows for closeness and blossoming and newness.

'Yes' understands that if there isn't energy for something, it won't happen anyway.

'Yes' allows for the fact that whatever is aligned with the aim, has space to grow, even if you can't see it at the outset.

'Yes' is a state of relief, of being free from having to determine everything, know everything, oversee everything, control anything.

When Not Saying No is the Problem

On the other side, one of the biggest problems women face is learning to say 'No'. I have a friend who always says 'Yes' to invitations, even when she knows that she won't go. Then she has to spend an inordinate amount of energy working out an excuse and a way to eventually say 'No'. But she has to lie to do it. We all know that she has to maintain this web of lies and that she will most likely drop out of engagements and agreements at the last minute. These lies are small things, however, maintaining a large series of lies requires a lot of energy and brain power and attention that could be better spent on other areas of life. It is easier and more respectful to yourself and others to learn to say 'No'.

Not being able to say *no* is a strong indication that we don't know ourselves or don't value ourselves. Putting other people's feelings and needs and desires ahead of our own, indicates that there are some healthy boundaries missing. Boundaries become extremely blurred in dysfunctional relationships – that is relationships where there is extreme attachment, dependency, co-dependency (enabling of each others' negative behaviour patterns). Boundaries are the edges of our personal space – our mental, emotional, physical and spiritual space. When these boundaries are transgressed regularly, we can easily forget that we have a right to have that space. We not only let others violate this space, but it is as if we put up a sign saying 'trespassers welcome'. Unfortunately this kind of invitation attracts damaging relationships, people whose survival patterns are of abuse – either subtle or extreme. No boundaries together with 'trespassers welcome', becomes a strategy for getting attention, approval, affection… basically meagre versions of the love we all need but don't feel able or worthwhile to get.

I have been working with a corporate executive who is very smart, caring, talented and has incredible capacity to learn and change, fast. Some of the work that we did at the beginning of our contract highlighted that she was 'too nice'. She had grown up in a family where there was chaos around her and it was her job to maintain the harmony in the family environment. This meant that her boundaries were definitely skewed. One of the main values that she carried forward into her adult life, was the value of being 'polite'.

When we started to analyse this politeness, it became clear that it was an imposition of someone else's idea of how she should behave. Don't cause any trouble, don't make anyone uncomfortable, don't say what you think, keep everything 'nice'. But in doing this, she was suppressing her own inner voice. Sometimes there's a voice telling you that this is not okay behaviour, that this person can't speak to you like this or treat you like this, and to be polite in this case is not valuing yourself. So we started to work with the concept that respect was a higher level value than being polite, which was very Traditional Face.

Respect means respect for yourself first. Your voice is valuable, your knowing is worthwhile, your experience is valid. Your values and boundaries are clear.

Then respect for others. This means treating them as human beings of value. Where there is respect, there can be honesty. Politeness rarely leaves space for honesty. This is a fundamental part of respect. It may be necessary to temper honesty and directness with the art of managing sensitivity and egos, but value yourself enough to be clear regarding what's acceptable and what's not, what's do-able and what's not, what's important and what's not.

Respect is a powerful space to come from. Polite is a weak and powerless place to be and to speak from.

This shift in a values filter gave my client a new way of seeing herself and of placing herself in her world of relationships and roles. It made an enormous difference to all aspects of her life. When you shift something in your own awareness, it naturally makes changes in your outer world that align.

Saying 'no' is a matter of self-respect, of replacing boundaries that have been removed, damaged, breached or abused. It takes practice, but it is worthwhile. Reclaiming boundaries is an act of self-love and self-value. In the journey back to wholeness, to your own 100 per cent pure self, re-establishing boundaries is a crucial step in re-establishing your own energetic domain...YOU.

SHAKTI MUST DISAPPEAR

Shakti is a reality and a role, but not a role to become attached to. Unlike the agent of change, the Modern Face, Shakti is an agent of *transformation*, which means that inherent in the role is her own destruction. That probably sounds very provocative, but perhaps I can explain a little more.

Unlike the Eternal Face, Shakti is a time-based Face. It is not eternal. It can be accessed, worn, and played out during times, and in particular, this *era* of transformation. The challenge is to adopt Shakti as a transitional role, not as an identity to become attached to. This a challenge, because this has been our way of living. Taking on a role, becoming the role, and losing ourselves to the role. Shakti is the method by which we return to ourselves, and once we have returned fully, the Face is redundant, irrelevant, unnecessary.

Shakti is the bearer of understanding of the process of transformation. It is the wise and powerful part of us who is constantly witness, observer to her own journey.

Shakti is the one who can rise above the magnetic pull of the Traditional and Modern Faces and not believe their cunning. She is the one who can work consciously with the 8 Powers to alleviate torment within her own soul and the souls of others. As the Great Mother, Shakti is the one who is the protector of her own innocence, her own purity of being. Once reclaimed, she becomes wise to the ways in which to maintain the sweetness and beauty she has recovered and she is ruthless in taking care of her prize.

Shakti is the conscious awareness of :

- Who we are
- Where we have come from
- The journey we are on
- The task that needs to be accomplished in the world at present

- What our individual part is within that
- How to perceive and manage our self-sabotaging survival patterns
- The role of God in a personal and universal sense that goes beyond religious belief.

... And all of this is a role that is transitional. As such, when we arrive at our destination of 'being' and supporting the 'being' of others, Shakti will die.

The challenge is not to attach to the role. The art is to play the role, but be the soul.

After years and lifetimes of having lost ourselves to roles and projected identities, the habit is very powerful. And yet it is dangerous, because if we are to do what the role, the face, is born to do, then she must be free to be victorious and then disappear.

The journey through the confluence – the convergence of the old and new – is the subtle and slippery realm of illusion. Along the way, throughout the journey, the old patterns of ego will slide across into the spiritual game and lure us into believing them to be real. We can be on a spiritual journey but still playing out old patterns.

Jason, a dear friend in Australia, first introduced me to the concept that the spiritual path is fundamentally different from the achievement model of the 20th and 21st Centuries. The achievement model proposes – and we have bought it – that who we are is not good enough, but that as soon as we become something 'other', better, where 'better' is constructed by the collective consciousness of the time, then and only then will we be enough.

Often when we start our spiritual journey we overlay this belief onto our practices and efforts. We have to be the best meditator, having the most powerful experiences, being the truest of heart, sweetest of nature, the clearest channel, the most popular teacher (with the least ego), the most disciplined, dedicated, honest, and so on. All in comparison to others, or an idealized self, measuring against an external criteria. Finding role models who inspire you, who provide a 'mirror' for you to see your own innate potential is another matter. However, adopting the same mental model, the achievement model, that caused us to lose ourselves before, is the antithesis of spiritual path. Comparison, competition, colluding with a belief that one day in the future I will be okay but until that day, I must work hard to change myself and only then maybe I will be worthy to be face to face with Divinity, with God.

Again this is the ego playing its fear and control games. The thing I love about spiritual development is that it starts from the basis that *Who I am is enough, if I could just be that more often.*

Personal development is about not being good enough and needing to become better. The paradox is that once I accept myself, everything changes anyway. Once I accept feelings of vulnerability, of aloneness, of fear, of uncertainty and so on, then I can start to make some choices and I move forward. When I deny, avoid, suppress, then I don't have choice, rather these unacknowledged energies will sabotage me at an unconscious level and will drive me, they will demand to be noticed, acting out, behaving badly, engaging addiction until they rise to a conscious level and are owned. Once owned, then and only then, do we start to have power over them. When hidden they are in charge, determining and directing all from the shadows.

Once embraced from a standpoint of 'Shakti' – the powerful observer position, then starts the journey of recovering our own power, strength, beauty, dignity, truth. This is a powerful place from which to learn.

Recently I met with a young man who is really struggling with his inner world, which is now affecting his work, relationship and wellbeing. He works in law and he is very unhappy. Well, that is how the conversation began. He asked me why he was comparing himself with other colleagues all the time and feeling himself to be less. His self-esteem was very low and his confidence, relationships and potentially his career, were suffering as a result. Every day he was going into work not as John, but as 'corporate law guy'. Apart from the fact that he really wanted to be growing berries, he had lost all sense of his own being. He was building an identity on shaky ground. As the lawyer, there was always someone better and someone worse than he. He was never at rest, at peace with who he was.

One has to ask the question: "If I reached the end of my life and all I could say was that I was the best (or 100th or 1000th best) corporate lawyer in the world" – would that be enough? Is that what this young man was born for? I don't think so. In fact I think he was suffering a mid-life crisis at 32 years of age.

This is promising. It means that if he listens to his 'soul' speaking to him, he will recognize that his sorrow is a signal and he will avert a major crisis in his forties or fifties. He can recover now, if he trusts his inner voice and moves forward asking questions like: "who am I?" and "what am I here for?"

I shared with him something that I had heard many years before that I still find incredibly useful.

If you want better answers, ask better questions.

Why am I not as good as him? Why am I not clever, beautiful, successful, admired, included, valued...? These questions take us to depleted answers, diminished possibilities. Learning to ask myself questions that give my intellect somewhere enquiring and new and positive to go, is a helpful tool in life.

"What signals might I see, that would indicate to me my purpose in life?"

"What do others admire in me?"

"If I knew I were to die in three months, how might that change my life?" And then: "What am I waiting for?

"If I am to stay awake on this path, what do I know about looking after my consciousness? My awareness? Myself?"

If you want better answers, ask better questions.

The Ego Survives

The ego will do all it can to survive. This is the work of the ego. When we lost our authentic identity, the ego emerged to enable us to survive day to day, albeit sometimes shakily. And we know what happens when survival is threatened. All resources, all defences are engaged. The ego will do its utmost to live on and will manipulate us in the cleverest of ways in order to survive.

You think you have risen to a higher consciousness, to a higher purpose and without realising, ego has slipped in and made you feel good about who you are because of what you are doing or have done. Now your identity is locked into being a 'good person', a 'light worker', an 'instrument for God'. However, if we take our sense of self from any label, then ego has won. No matter how valuable the label is. I know this first hand.

I was in Chile, a guest, a visitor. I was there for one week but due to an emergency hysterectomy, a week became five months, and is now a year and half as I sit here writing this.

In the first few months I was so happy. I was useful. My life was balanced. My spiritual world was so strong, my meditation was easy, lovely, powerful and sweet at all times, even with a tiny amount of sleep. I was exercising regularly and enjoying it. I was unattached to any outcomes. I was loving, I was supportive, and my vision was clean. All the things I had learned in my life were available for use if needed. And I was blessed in that there were a range of things that were useful to the community where I was staying. My Shakti role of transformation was working well, I was not imposing myself but being available for God's work, guided in the moment through a silent and peaceful mind. Until...

The ego took hold and claimed the Shakti as it is own. I became attached to the role of transformer. And it was so subtle that I didn't realize that it was happening until it had destroyed the sublime experience of the beauty and harmony, returning me to something more ordinary.

So I am in the process now of being kind to myself, of

attempting to recover the magic of Being on a constant and permanent basis. Of being responsible but not taking on the burden of responsibility. Of doing the job and then slipping away. Of taking all my nourishment from the Source and not from the results.

So it is important to understand that we will be hijacked, that we will lose the round from time to time. Ego is a well-oiled master of manipulation, it has been the way of surviving when we didn't know any other way. So it will certainly know or learn every trick possible to keep going. That's its job, its role, its raison d'etre.

So keep moving, while paradoxically staying still. Redefining – allowing each new moment to bring forth something new. Letting Go. Remembering that we are never lost if we can stay awake, aware and kind, tender with ourselves.

Non-Judgment

When we accept that we will forget and that we will fall foul to survival patterns, when we understand that this is the way of things, then it is possible to employ the alchemical tool of non-judgment.

If being able to stay awake and be detached is the first step, then the second is non-judgement.

When I was turning 40, I decided that I didn't want another decade of intensity and introspection. I had been so heavy and harsh with myself in my bid for perfection, so judgemental. I was caught in the achievement model, and with every harsh verdict that I gave myself, I lost confidence and hope and energy.

I remember four gems told to me during those years by my spiritual mentor Dadi Janki:

- You think too much
- If you're not experiencing happiness, then you have the wrong method

- Don't ask why, it will only take you into sorrow.
- You think too much (again!)

So I practiced not thinking so much. It was difficult but I practiced. And it was helpful. I found that by controlling my ceaseless random thoughts, I was able to use my facility for thinking for more useful things. I could strengthen my intellect with interesting and inspiring thoughts and consciously choose to not engage in the rubbish, the negative, the waste.

Intellectually I understood that if I wasn't experiencing happiness I must have the wrong method, but I didn't truly understand that this harsh self-criticism was a faulty method. In fact, I didn't diagnose it as a method at all. I thought this was the way of things.

I had learned to 'check and change'. Check myself and then change what isn't true, real, beautiful. Good strategy for evolution but not if accompanied by castigation! In order to change we have to have energy and confidence and self-belief and a positive, loving environment. A flower grows with nurture, care and the right conditions. A child grows with nurture, care and encouragement. How could I possibly have thought that to psychologically, spiritually or emotionally flagellate myself would produce a positive result? But I did. And many, many others do too.

A very dear friend was instrumental in helping me turn this pattern over forever. One New Year's eve, we were talking, reflecting on the way of things and the year that had passed. I was feeling a little melancholy that another year had gone and still I hadn't achieved the level of spirituality that I thought I should have achieved.

My friend is a very sensible character, and his philosophy is the 'art of the long view'. He is very clear on his aim, the return to his own absolute truth, and he moves forward consistently, day by day, toward that truth. But if on the way there are slight aberrations, he doesn't mind, he doesn't get caught up, he understands that this is the way of things and just keeps moving.

So there I was feeling sorry for myself and in reflection I must admit, expecting a little sympathy from my good friend. As I talked on, he seemed to become more distant, more cool. Then with total detachment, and a lot of love, I heard this question.

"Why do you do this to yourself?"

"Do what?"

"This. Beat up on yourself like this. You're such a good soul and you give yourself such a hard time. I mean, if it worked, fine. But clearly, it doesn't. I think you'd better find yourself a new method."

In this one defining moment I was both shocked and liberated. Shocked that someone so close to me could be so detached and direct. And liberated, because someone so close to me could be so detached and direct.

Since that time, I have been a full-time student in the art of gentleness and kindness. Firstly to myself. I have discovered that if I am kind and tolerant with myself, then I am more likely to be so with others. If I treat myself with disdain and loathing and harsh judgment, then I am likely to pull others into hell with me.

As with everything there is a balance to be learned, harmonising and integrating of polarities to be done. Kindness and love and tenderness are nicely balanced with commitment, courage and firmness.

Choices and Consequences

Long gone is the fire and brimstone, guilt-based living of my religious upbringing. But I do find it very useful to understand that there are consequences to choices.

On a spiritual path, the further you travel, the more you recognise and feel the consequences of thoughts and actions. If you are not in alignment with your own truth, you will be uncertain, insecure, anxious – even if only subtly. This insecurity will cause self-centred thinking and actions – survival behaviour.

This has become normal, but it carries with it a string of unwanted consequences. Insecurity will always lead us to make choices focused on self-preservation, which shrinks our world. Our lives reduce in stamina and generosity, in love and hope, and possibility. When there is fear, there are opponents and enemies. Trust is impaired. Vision is narrowed. Choices are poor. Consequences are poor. Our lives become impoverished.

So in order to move forward expanding into life with a sense of opening and abundance, it is critical to know oneself and practice trusting the 'I', learning to rest in your Being, because choices made from your truth will always carry consequences that are creative, powerful and positive.

This is the aim. This is the reason for the Shakti to exist… to return us to this natural state of pure alignment, of unfettered creative living, of harmonious and peaceful living. Once returned, the Shakti's time is over, her role is obsolete. Her job is done. She disappears…until next time.

AFTERWORD

I would like to finish with this prophecy reported from indigenous elders in North America. It speaks in such a direct, poetic and inspiring way about the time we are in and the people we are. I hope you find solace and encouragement in the words below.

Hopi Elders' Prophecy
Oraibi, Arizona, June 8, 2000

You have been telling people that this is the Eleventh Hour.
Now you must go back and tell the people that this is the Hour.
And there are things to be considered . . .

Where are you living?
What are you doing?
What are your relationships?
Are you in right relation?
Where is your water?

Know your garden.
It is time to speak your truth.
Create your community.
Be good to each other.
And do not look outside yourself for your leader.

Then he clasped his hands together, smiled, and said, "This could be a good time! There is a river flowing now very fast. It is so great and swift that there are those who will be afraid. They will try to hold on to the shore. They will feel they are being torn apart and will suffer greatly. Know the river has its destination. The elders say we must let go of the shore, push off into the middle of the river, keep our eyes open, and our heads above the water.

And I say, see who is in there with you and celebrate. At this time in history, we are to take nothing personally, least of all ourselves. For the moment that we do, our spiritual growth and journey come to a halt.

The time of the one wolf is over. Gather yourselves! Banish the word 'struggle' from your attitude and your vocabulary. All that we do now must be done in a sacred manner and in celebration.

We are the ones we've been waiting for."

NOTES

1 The 8 Powers of the Shakti – Withdraw, Let Go, Tolerate, Accept, Discern, DECIDE, Face, Cooperate. In the chapter on Shakti, there are seven different ways of working with each of the 8 Powers.

2 Mind maps are very useful tools for getting your thoughts and feelings out of your amorphous inner world. They help create some structure that makes it easier to see the whole picture. Mapping is not a linear 'listing' process which always omits significant components of a whole experience. Mapping is inclusive and puts on paper all the parts and the interconnectedness of those parts. In the middle of the page in a circle you put the idea, the thought, the feeling, the topic. Then like a spider's web, you draw lines outward, linking to other circles that carry connected thoughts and ideas. From those, you link to other connected thoughts, feelings or impressions.

BOOKS

mySpiritRadio

7 Aha's of Highly Enlightened Souls
Mike George

A very profound, self empowering book. Each page bursting with wisdom and insight. One you will need to read and reread over and over again! **Paradigm Shift**

1903816319 128pp £5.99 $11.95

Don't Get MAD Get Wise
Why no one ever makes you angry!
Mike George

After "The Power of Now", I thought I would never find another self-help book that was even a quarter as useful as that. I was wrong. Mike George's book on anger, like a Zen master's teaching, is simple yet profound. This isn't one of those wishy-washy books about forgiving people. It's just the opposite....a spiritually powerful little book. **Marian Van Eyk**, *Living Now Magazine*

1905047827 160pp £7.99 $14.95

Celtic Wheel of the Year, The
Celtic and Christian Seasonal Prayers
Tess Ward

This book is highly recommended. It will make a perfect gift at any time of the year. There is no better way to conclude than by quoting the cover endorsement by Diarmuid O'Murchu MSC, "Tess Ward writes like a mystic. *A gem for all seasons!' It is a gem indeed.* **Revd. John Churcher**, Progressive Christian Network

1905047959 304pp £11.99 $21.95

Savage Breast
Tim Ward

An epic, elegant, scholarly search for the goddess, weaving together travel, Greek mythology, and personal autobiographic relationships into a remarkable exploration of the Western World's culture and sexual history. It is also entertainingly human, as we listen and learn from this accomplished person and the challenging mate he wooed. If you ever travel to Greece, take "Savage Breast" along with you. **Harold Schulman**, Professor of Gynaecology at Winthrop University Hospital, and author of *An Intimate History of the Vagina*

1905047584 400pp £12.99 $19.95

A Global Guide to Interfaith
Reflections From Around the World
Sandy Bharat

This amazing book gives a wonderful picture of the variety and excitement of this journey of discovery. **Rev Dr. Marcus Braybrooke**, President of the World Congress of Faiths

1905047975 336pp £19.99 $34.95

Everyday Buddha
Lawrence Ellyard

Whether you already have a copy of the Dhammapada or not, I recommend you get this. If you are new to Buddhism this is a great place

to start. The whole feel of the book is lovely, the layout of the verses is clear and the simple illustrations are very beautiful, catching a feel for the original work. His Holiness the Dalai Lama's foreword is particularly beautiful, worth the purchase price alone. Lawrence's introduction is clear and simple and sets the context for what follows without getting bogged down in information... I congradulate all involved in this project and have put the book on my recommended list. **Nova Magazine**

1905047304 144pp **£9.99 $19.95**

Peace Prayers
From the World's Faiths
Roger Grainger

Deeply humbling. This is a precious little book for those interested in building bridges and doing something practical about peace. **Odyssey**

1905047665 144pp **£11.99 $19.95**

Shamanic Reiki
Expanded Ways of Workling with Universal Life Force Energy
Llyn Roberts and Robert Levy

The alchemy of shamanism and Reiki is nothing less than pure gold in the hands of Llyn Roberts and Robert Levy. Shamanic Reiki brings the concept of energy healing to a whole new level. More than a how-to-book, it speaks to the health of the human spirit, a journey we must all complete. **Brian Luke Seaward**, Ph.D., author of *Stand Like Mountain, Flow Like Water, Quiet Mind, Fearless Heart*

9781846940378 208pp **£9.99 $19.95**

The Good Remembering
A Message for our Times
Llyn Roberts

Llyn's work changed my life. "The Good Remembering" is the most important book I've ever read. **John Perkins**, *NY Times* best selling author of *"Confessions of an Economic Hit Man"*

1846940389 96pp £7.99 $16.95

The Last of the Shor Shamans
Alexander and Luba Arbachakov

The publication of Alexander and Luba Arbachakov's 2004 study of Shamanism in their own community in Siberia is an important addition to the study of the anthropology and sociology of the peoples of Russia. Joanna Dobson's excellent English translation of the Arbachakov's work brings to a wider international audience a fascinating glimpse into the rapidly disappearing traditional world of the Shor Mountain people. That the few and very elderly Shortsi Shamans were willing to share their beliefs and experiences with the Arbachakov's has enabled us all to peer into this mysterious and mystic world. **Frederick Lundahl**, retired American Diplomat and specialist on Central Asia

9781846941276 96pp £9.99 $19.95

Thoughtful Guide to God
Howard Jones

As thoughtful as the title claims, this is thorough, with excellent background, history and depth, and is just right for the kind of person who sees, feels and perhaps has already begun to find the fusion of

consciousness that shows the way out of the confusion of our times towards a way of being that is positive, without being naive, and profoundly informative, without being pedantic. If you have a brain, heart and soul, and the interest to see where they become one, this book is a must. **Odyssey**

1905047703 400pp **£19.99 $39.95**

The Thoughtful Guide to Religion
Why it began, how it works, and where it's going
Ivor Morrish

A massive amount of material, clearly written, readable and never dry. the fruit of a lifetime's study, a splendid book. It is a major achievement to cover so much background in a volume compact enough to read on the bus. Morris is particularly good on illustrating the inter-relationships betwen religions. I found it hard to put down. **Faith and Freedom**

190504769X 384pp **£24.99 $34.95**

Life in Paradox
The Story of a Gay Catholic Priest
Paul Edward Murray

This memoir is the compelling story of an honest, sensitive priest, and the tragic tale of a hierarchy that has lost its way in its desire to control the Church rather than nurture it. No book sets out more clearly and urgently the tragedy and the prospects of the current crisis of Catholicism. **Bruce Chilton**, Bernard Iddings Bell Professor of Religion, Bard College

9781846941122 240pp **£11.99 $24.95**

Wojtyla's Women
How Women, History and Polish Traditions Shaped the Life of Pope John Paul II and Changed the Catholic Church
Ted Lipien

An important book. Few persons are as qualified as he is to enlighten readers about Pope John Paul II's Polish roots – and the impact that they had on his views on women. Lipien provides a stimulating analysis of the Pope's ideas on gender roles and how John Paul believed the Church should deal with sexual issues. This is a must-read for anyone interested in the relationship between feminism and Catholicism, a key issue of our times. **Dr. John H. Brown**, editor of *"Public Diplomacy Press Review"*

9781846941108 688pp £14.99 $29.95

The First English Prayer Book (Adapted for Modern Use)
The first worship edition since the original publication in 1549
Robert Van de Weyer

In 1549 Thomas Cranmer published the first Prayer Book in English. Based on a medieval form of worship, its language is both sublime and majestic. This new edition presents Cranmer's services in a form which is practical, accessible and easy to follow.

9781846941306 160pp £9.99 $19.95

Who Is Right About God?
Thinking Through Christian Attitudes in a World of Many Faiths
Duncan Raynor

This book is both important and readable, because it has been forged in the daily "real time" interplay between the issues and views that it discusses, and because it is given rigour and intellectual coherence by the gifted author, who has an Oxford training in philosophy, as well as theology. **The Very Revd Robert Grimley**, Dean of Bristol Cathedral

9781846941030 144pp **£11.99 $24.95**

The Other Buddhism
Amida Comes West
Caroline Brazier

An essential book for Buddhists, for students of religion, and for therapists of all schools, and for anyone who seeks an improved ability to cope with the stresses of our everyday world. **Jim Pym**, editor of *Pure Land Notes*

978-1-84694-0 304pp **£11.99 $24.95**

The Way Things Are
A Living Approach to Buddhism
Lama Ole Nydahl

It is my wish that through this book, the seed of Buddhahood is planted in the reader's mind. By putting the teachings presented here into practice, may they accomplish the ultimate goal of Enlightenment for the benefit of all. **Trinlay Thaye Dorje**, the 17th Gyalwa Karmapa

1846940427 192pp **£9.99 $19.95**

Who Loves Dies Well
On the Brink of Buddha's Pure Land
David Brazier

Practical, moving and full of deep love for the reader, and as such is the perfect guide to newcomers and experienced Buddhists alike. **Jim Pym**, author of *You Don't Have to Sit on the Floor.*

9781846940453 256pp **£11.99 $19.95**

The House of Wisdom
Yoga of the East and West
Swami Dharmananda Saraswati and Santoshan

Swamiji has shared her wisdom with her students for many years. Now her profound and enlightening writings, and those of Santoshan, are made available to a wider audience in this excellent book. The House of Wisdom is a real treasure-house of spiritual knowledge. **Priya Shakti (Julie Friedeberger)**, author of *The Healing Power of Yoga*

1846940249 224pp **£11.99 $22.95**